advance praise

"It is unusual when two good friends create a convergence of deep Christian commitment, immense giftedness for ministry, apostolic vision, and the ability to write well so that their ministries may be multiplied for the glory of God. Andy and Lowell are two such persons. Lowell, the evangelistic pastor of a great, growing church with a heart for mission, and Andy, the traveling evangelist with a genius for reaching persons of all ages, are a perfect pair to teach and inspire us all. Read this book and practice what it preaches. God will bless you for it!"

—Rev. Dr. Harold Bales, former director, Evangelization Development for the General Board of Discipleship

"Reading this book is an excellent way for 'youth' of any age to begin their faith journey or to get refueled—practical, instructive, challenging, and very personal with more than just a touch of humor thrown in! Lowell and Andy take you to the heart of a personal understanding of the Gospel and on to forming life-changing spiritual habits."

—Katie Fralic, director of youth and young adult ministries, Western NC Conference

"For Christians who are seeking solid food to grow in Christ, this book is an all-you-can-eat spiritual buffet!"

—Kipp Garrett, youth pastor

"This is a wonderful and hilarious guide that is guaranteed to keep your attention while keeping you strongly rooted in the Word. This message is great for all Christians—old or new."

—Allison Barnes, graduate student

"Wow! This book is awesome. Fuel for the Journey really lays out the essentials of a relationship with Christ. I found myself laughing at Lowell and Andy's ridiculous stories, but at the same time deepening my understanding of what it means to be a Christian. This book will serve as a great tool for a group that wants to explore Christianity together."

—Ben Masten, high school student

fuel for the journey ›››

a daily guide for new
& growing Christians

lowell McNANEY & andy LAMBERT

Fuel for the Journey: A Daily Guide for New and Growing Christians
by Lowell McNaney and Andy Lambert

Text copyright © 2003 by Lowell McNaney and Andy Lambert
Illustrations copyright © 2003 by K. Scott Whitaker

First edition 2003
09 08 07 06 05 04 03   7 6 5 4 3 2 1
ISBN 1-930154-11-9

Book design and production by Whitline Ink Incorporated
PO Box 668, 114 S. Carolina Avenue, Boonville, NC 27011
whitlineink@yadtel.net ——————— (336)367-6914

If you have any questions or comments about this book, want to order additional copies, or want to find out about bulk order discounts, contact us directly by e-mail or in writing:

e-mail: fuelforthejourney@hotmail.com
write: Isaac Ministries, P.O. Box 275, Boonville, NC 27011

Printed in the United States of America

lowell's dedication >>>

I dedicate this book to my Lord and Savior Jesus Christ. Thank You for Your grace, Your provision, and Your incredible sacrifice. I live eternally grateful.

And to Jennifer, my beautiful wife, my teammate in ministry, the one who makes my heart go hubba-hubba, my crown, and my friend. Thank you for believing in a skinny little preacher and for your Ruth-like willingness to be my companion wherever God has led us. There's no one I would rather be running the race with than you.

To my daughters, Rebekah, Cassie, and Aleia. In my completely unbiased opinion, you are without a doubt the three coolest girls in the world. I am so very proud of you.

To my parents, Treva and Bill McNaney, the most courageous woman and the kindest man I ever knew.

To my brother, Mike. I am so thankful that you have also become my brother in the faith.

To my in-laws, Dennis, Linda, and Doug Greyshock. Thank you for always making me feel like family.

To the wonderful people of Crossroads. Thank you for being so much more than the church I have the privilege of serving and for being my fellow workers in the Vineyard. Thank you for being my friends.

To my friends throughout the years who have blessed my life, lightened my burden, lifted my arms, and brightened my path.

To all those who passionately wish to love, know, and serve the King of Kings. You know who you are.

andy's dedication >>>

This book is dedicated to...
Christ, who set me on a new path, and every day provides fuel for the journey.

To my wife, Renee. Words cannot do justice for how much I love you. Thank you for holding down the homefront while I'm on the road.

To my daughters, Grace and Joy. You are the delights of my life.

Finally, and with great admiration, I dedicate this book in memory of my father-in-law, Carl Poplin.

fuel for the journey › › ›

contents > > >

SECTION 6 >

Being Stewards of What God Has Given Us

SECTION 7 >

How God Guides Us in Our Big Decisions and Daily Lives

SECTION 8 >

Victory Over Daily Struggles

fuel for the journey › › ›

i n t r o > > >

I leaned against the edge of the stage at the close of what had been a powerful youth event. I was simultaneously exhausted and exhilarated. Half of the bustling crowd headed toward the exits in order to stuff hastily packed suitcases in already overly stuffed church vans. The other half lingered to pray or say their goodbyes. In the midst of this hoard of humanity, a teenager grabbed my arm. With tear-filled eyes and a beaming countenance, he announced to me, "I want you to know that I just gave my life to Christ."

Before I could say a word, however, a youth counselor spun me around and frantically pleaded, "Please come pray with one of my youth."

"One second and I'll be right there," I said as I wheeled back toward the new Christian in order to finish our conversation. But when I turned, the young man was nowhere to be found. He had disappeared into the herd of highly hormonal humans headed home.

Although my feet were following the counselor in order to pray with her heartbroken youth, my thoughts were on the nameless teen who had vanished. Would his faith disappear in the crowded activities of his life? Would he tell his parents or his pastor about his encounter with Christ this weekend? Would anybody be praying for him? Would there be anyone to encourage him in the faith? Did he know anything about the importance of having a prayer life or personal Bible study? My experience with the disappearing new believer can be viewed as an analogy of a worldwide problem: **Far too many people come to an experience with Christ and then disappear into the crowd.** Therefore, a driving passion in producing this book was to place a tool in the hands of new believers that would encourage and develop their new faith.

This book is not only for new believers, however. Earlier this week, we received a letter from a woman who had recently started coming to our church. Her correspondence went something like this:

> "I feel like I am lacking the basics of the faith. I need a 'Christianity 101' for adults, and/or, I hate to be crass, but 'The Complete Idiots Guide to Christianity.'...I'd like to move forward in my faith journey, but I feel stuck in grammar school."

The lady who wrote this is not a new believer; she has attended church since childhood. She is also not alone. Her letter sums up the frustrations of numerous individuals who feel uninformed and in the dark concerning the foundations of the faith as well as those things necessary to grow and thrive as a Christian. For those who can relate to this woman's hunger and frustration, we pray this book is of assistance to you as well.

There is another category of believers to which we hope these devotions will be beneficial: the rest of us who simply need periodically to be reminded of the basics. When the Lord takes us to a new level with Him, many times He does so by leading us back to the essentials. After a couple of poorly played games, Coach Vince Lombardi once had his Green Bay Packers take a knee on the sideline. He pulled out a ball from a bag and said, "Gentlemen, this is a football. It is made out of leather, and you will notice that it has laces on one side. The game is also called football and it is played on a field one-hundred yards long with two ten-yard end zones. The field is laid out in ten-yard increments. The object of the game of football is to..."

He went on to discuss the ABCs of blocking, tackling, running with the football, and so on. Mind you, he was talking to professionals who had been playing the game since childhood. What happened as a result of Vince's detailed discourse? The Packers went undefeated for the remainder of the season, including the playoffs. In addition, one player who was present that day, and who would go on to be inducted into the Football Hall of Fame, pointed to that speech as the changing point in his career. It was when he was reminded of the basics that he was enabled to take his game to another level. So, for all of you seasoned vets, we pray that the things contained in this book will help you "remember your First Love," "do the things you did at first," and take your game to a higher level.

>   >   >

On returning home from another youth weekend retreat, I saw a church van pulled over on the side of the road. I recognized from the logo on the vehicle and the tuckered teenagers crammed inside as "retreaters" retreating home. When I pulled over to see if I could help, the embarrassed leaders informed me that there was nothing wrong with the vehicle. They simply ran out of gas.

Sadly, far too many people make decisions for Christ, yet run out of gas on the way home. No athlete or vehicle can work without fuel. Neither can a Christian. A believer cannot continue to grow and thrive today on yesterday's manna. If our mountaintop moment is not followed with down-to-earth discipleship, what will result is a tired, miserable, watered downed, and barren version of "Christianity."

> > >

Before you proceed, here are some words of clarification:

- In the hope of keeping you interested, as well as for your enjoyment, we have written in a variety of styles and formats.
- This book is not intended to be devoured in one sitting but to be savored in daily doses.
- Although you'll find scripture throughout these pages, we have set aside within each devotion a section titled **FUEL**, in which we focus on specific biblical passages so you can receive the "high octane" truth directly from the Word of God.
- Most devotions also have a section entitled **reACTION**. It is our sincere desire that your *reaction* to each highlighted topic will lead to *actions* in your life.
- Because we wrote the vast majority of this book bouncing ideas (and projectiles) off one another, we do not identify which lines belong to Lowell or which anecdotes came from Andy. *(Hint: I wrote most of the good stuff.)*

This book is not meant to replace a loving church, a godly pastor, or the friendship and accountability of other believers. Instead, one of the intentions of this book is to point you toward all those vital means of experiencing Christ in a deeper way and to give you FUEL FOR THE JOURNEY.

—Andy Lambert and Lowell McNaney

prologue > > >

First Things First

"I remember two things: that I am a great sinner and that Christ is a great Savior."   —John Newton, author of "Amazing Grace"

"One thief on the cross was saved, that none should despair; and only one, that none should presume."
                                                                    —J.C. Ryle

From the moment your alarm clock blares, life's questions begin: How many times can I hit the snooze button? How many times have I already hit the snooze button? What did that dream about purple penguins flying out of my left nostril mean? Where are my socks? Do I rinse and repeat or throw caution to the wind and just rinse? Sugar-coated doughnuts or bark-filled granola for breakfast? What am I going to wear? Do these socks make me look fat? CNN or Looney Tunes?

Throughout the day our brains are continually bombarded with both life-changing, significant questions and mindless, tedious inquiries. Paper or plastic? Who will I marry? Linguini or lasagna for lunch? Does my life have a purpose? Is that a penguin pellet on my pillow? Why do good people suffer? Did I already put on deodorant? What's for supper?

Two thousand years ago, a Roman correctional officer crawled out of bed and began what initially appeared to be just another ordinary day filled with ordinary questions: I wonder if it's supposed to be cold today? How do I get to work, camel or chariot? Do these sandals make me look fat? Why hasn't anyone invented deodorant? Will my family have enough food? At midnight, however, after this prison guard had an encounter with the power of the living God, this ordinary man posed an extraordinary question. In fact, he asked life's most important inquiry:

"What must I do to be saved?" (Acts 16:30)

Everything hinges on the answer to this question. Our purpose in this life, as well as our eternal destiny, rests in our understanding of and our response to God's answer to this vital question. We realize that the majority of this book's readers are either new or growing Christians. Furthermore, many of you might still be searching or have questions about your faith, and are seeking answers as to how one receives God's salvation. This being the case, we will do our best to present the path to salvation in a clear and understandable way.

There are five essential steps in receiving God's awesome gift:

1› **Realize God's incredible love for you and His incredible purpose for your life.**
2› **Recognize your condition apart from God.**
3› **Rely on Christ's finished work on the cross.**
4› **Repent of your sins.**
5› **Receive Christ as the Lord and Savior of your life.**

‹ 1 ›

Realize God's incredible love for you and His incredible purpose for your life.

"For God so loved the world that he gave his one and only Son, that whoever believes in Him shall not perish but have eternal life."

—John 3:16–17

"[B]e absolutely certain that our Lord loves you, devotedly and individually, loves you just as you are. …Accustom yourself to the wonderful thought that God loves you with a tenderness, a generosity, and an intimacy that surpasses all your dreams." —Abbe Henri de Tourville

Contrary to Darwin, you are not a random genetic accident of a cold, impersonal universe. Instead, you are a masterpiece, designed and created by an awesome, personal God. This incredible God created you in order that He might know you, befriend you, and, most of all, love you. In addition, your Designer has a wonderful design for your life. There is more to your existence than a dash between two dates on a headstone. He didn't make you simply to communicate, procreate, recreate, and asphyxiate. In other words, your awesome God has an awesome purpose and plan for your life.

"I have loved you with an everlasting love; I have drawn you with loving-kindness."
　　　　　　　　　　　　　　　　　　　　　—Jeremiah 31:3

"Nails didn't hold Jesus to the Cross, love did."
　　　　　　　　　　　　　　　　　　　　　—Max Lucado

"I praise you because I am fearfully and wonderfully made."
　　　　　　　　　　　　　　　　　　　　　—Psalm 139:14

"'For I know the plans I have for you,' declares the LORD, 'plans to prosper you and not to harm you, plans to give you hope and a future.'"
　　　　　　　　　　　　　　　　　　　　　—Jeremiah 29:11

‹ 2 ›

Recognize your condition apart from God.

"Dear Sir: Regarding your article 'What's Wrong with the World?' I am. Yours truly, G.K. Chesterton."
　　　　　　　　　　　　　　　　　　　　　—G.K. Chesterton

The opossums in the South have apparently joined together in a suicide pact. You can drive on any road in the South and find several recently deceased marsupials lying on or beside the pavement. Opossums obviously have a death wish. What else could account for their vain attempt to stop a rapidly approaching vehicle by staring it down and then ramming it with their cranium? Imagine going up to one of these departed dodos and attempting to spiffy it up a bit. You could put a diamond-studded watch on its tiny wrist, paint on a smiley face, dress it in some little opossum o-pants, or even style its hair with an opossum o-permanent. Do these activities help Mr. Opossum in any way? No, Mr. Opossum doesn't need a makeover. Mr. Opossum needs a resurrection.

Likewise, the Bible doesn't say that we are *sick* in our sin or that we have a *problem* with sin. God's Word declares in Ephesians 2:1, *"As for you, you were dead in your transgressions and sins."* In other words, our souls don't need spiffying up; we need a resurrection. We don't need a doctor; we need a Savior.

"The knowledge of God without that of our wretchedness creates pride. The knowledge of our wretchedness without that of God creates despair. The knowledge of Jesus Christ is the middle way, because in Him we find both God and our wretchedness."
—Blaise Pascal

Apart from Christ, we are not only dead in our sins, but we are also separated from God. If you have ever been to or seen pictures of the Grand Canyon, you realize that it is one serious hole in the ground. The canyon averages a whopping nine miles across. Can anyone jump across an expanse that wide? Not a chance. Even the world record long jump would come up around 47,000 feet short. One would truly have to have sushi for brains to attempt leaping across the canyon's breadth.

Because God is completely holy, sin creates a pit of impurity as big as the Grand Canyon between God and us. Sin is even more contrary to God's personality than purity is to ours. In addition, God cannot just wink at sin or shrug it off; otherwise, He would no longer be either holy or just. We are not talking about a separation that can easily be skipped across, but a distance so wide as to necessitate outside intervention in order to span it. Yet, amazingly, many people believe they can cross this chasm by their own effort. **Here are some of the more popular misconceptions:**

Salvation by S I N C E R I T Y

It's amazing how many people in our current culture hold to the creed, "It doesn't matter what you believe as long as you're sincere." Is that true? A friend of mine worked in a mental institution where a man was convinced he was Abraham Lincoln. Did his sincerity transform him into Honest Abe? No. If I sincerely believe that gravity has no effect on me and I decide to jump off the Eiffel Tower, will my sincerity keep me airborne? No. People will be scraping my sincerity off the cement with a putty knife. It is not enough to be sincere; we can be sincerely wrong. Our sincerity must be grounded in truth.

Salvation by C O M P A R I S O N

Our human tendency to compare ourselves to others often spills over into our beliefs about getting into heaven. We look at Suzie and think, "Hey, I'm a better person than she." Then we consider Al Capone and Adolf Hitler and think, "And I'm much better than they." We mistakenly assume that God grades on a curve. So in this line of thinking, it only makes sense that as long as we're better than half the population, we "pass" and are, therefore, heaven-bound.

The problem with the above assumption is that God makes it clear in His Word that He doesn't grade in this manner. Romans 3:23 tells us, *"for all have sinned and fall short of the glory of God."* Likewise, Romans 3:10 declares, *"There is no one righteous, not even one."* That means that instead of grading on a curve, God's grading scale is pass/fail, and unfortunately, He has declared that we all fail in our own effort.

"Heaven goes by favor. If it went by merit, you would stay out, and your dog would go in."

—Mark Twain

Salvation by S U B T R A C T I O N

This is the belief that, "If I don't do this and don't do that, then God will be pleased with me, and He'll let me into heaven. By sheer effort and will power, I'm going to stop cussing, drinking, lying, cheating, stealing, envying, lusting, holding grudges, and harassing my little brother."

Again, there are holes in this line of thinking. Do you honestly believe you could go even twenty-four hours without doing, saying, or thinking anything bad? How about twenty-four minutes? And what happens when we do blow it? (Notice I didn't say *if* we blow it.) Then what do we do with our sin? Furthermore, what do we do with the sin we already have? Can we ever be so good that we subtract all that sin away? No. Do the math: Salvation by subtraction doesn't add up.

"I [Paul] know that nothing good lives in me, that is, in my sinful nature. For I have the desire to do what is good, but I cannot carry it out. For what I do is not the good I want to do; no, the evil I do not want to do—this I keep on doing. What a wretched man I am! Who will rescue me from this body of death? Thanks be to God—through Jesus Christ our Lord!"

—Romans 7:18–19, 24–25

Salvation by S E R V I C E

"For it is by grace you have been saved, through faith—and this not from yourselves, it is the gift of God—not by works, so that no one can boast."

—Ephesians 2:8–9

People who hold to this faulty concept believe that if they perform enough good deeds (i.e. helping little old ladies across the street, going to church, praying, giving to the church or a worthy cause, and volunteering time and service), they will earn enough brownie points to be worthy of heaven. While these actions are well and good, these deeds aren't going to bridge the gap. Most of us would consider Billy Graham or Mother Teresa the ultimate examples of people deserving "salvation by service," yet they were convinced that their "acts of righteousness" were completely insufficient to blot out their sins or warrant entrance into the heaven of a perfect and holy God.

One of the starkest differences between Christianity and every other world religion is this: In every other faith, humanity attempts to climb the ladder of their own righteousness in the hope that, if they somehow make it to the top, they might possibility be accepted. The unique aspect to Christianity is this: God loves us so much, He abandoned the top rung and met us at the bottom. In other words, our salvation is based not on what we have done for Christ, but on what He has done for us.

"...He saved us, not because of righteous things we had done, but because of his mercy."
                                                            —Titus 3:5

‹ 3 ›

Rely on Christ's finished work on the cross.

When I was thirteen, I briefly bused tables at a fish restaurant. On my first day, I deftly balanced twenty or so glasses of iced tea on a tray, holding the tray with only my right hand. As I weaved my way through the maze of tables and about half way to my destination, I heard the gentle clink of two glasses nudging each other. The next thing I knew, the glasses, apparently taking cues from their suicidal opossum buddies, began careening off the side of the tray, shattering on the flounder-encrusted floor. Embarrassed but still alive, I cleaned up the mess and apologized to the manager.

He eased my fears by telling me not to worry, that accidents happen all the time in the restaurant business. He also informed me he had lost count of how many dishes and glasses he had personally had a hand in destroying. I thanked him for his understanding, but as I was walking away

I heard him say, "Of course, you know you're still going to have to pay for all those broken glasses." As a thirteen year old on my first day of work, I had to borrow money from my father to pay my debt. I learned a valuable lesson that day about how the universe works. When something gets broken, somebody has to pay for it.

Similarly, every lie and every lust, every wrong thought or twisted motive, every unkind word or neglected opportunity for kindness, is a transgression of God's moral law. His law has been broken, and somebody has to pay. The bad news is that this is a debt we can never personally pay. Furthermore, the first half of Romans 6:23 tells us, *"...the wages of sin is death."* Because we, as the human race and as individuals, have broken God's law, we deserve eternal death. The great news is this: God sent His only Son to die on the cross for our sins in order to pay that debt in full.

"For Christ died for sins once for all, the righteous for the unrighteous, to bring you to God."
—1 Peter 3:18

< 4 >

Repent of your sins.

"If we claim to be without sin, we deceive ourselves and the truth is not in us. If we confess our sins, he is faithful and just and will forgive us our sins and purify us from all unrighteousness."
—1 John 1:8–9

"Repentance is the process by which we see ourselves, day by day, as we really are: sinful, needy, dependent people. It is the process by which we see God as he is: awesome, majestic, and holy."
—Charles Colson

I thought to myself, Who is that redneck? In the next room my family was watching an old video we had filmed one Christmas. A particular voice on the video was so shrill that it could loosen dental fillings in Outer Mongolia. The voice sounded like a combination of a dying seal, Gomer Pyle, fighting cats, and fingernails being raked across a chalkboard. To my dismay, I soon realized that Gomer, the dying seal-cat, was me.

Most people cringe when looking at pictures of themselves or hearing their recorded voice. Who among us hasn't viewed a personal photo and questioned, "Is that my nose, or has a shark fin suddenly grown out of my face?" Okay, maybe you haven't dealt with that particular flaw (heaven "nose" we have!), but you get the idea. Regardless of the imperfection, facing our physical faults is never fun. If looking at our physical blemishes is that painful to us, is it any wonder that we do all we can to dodge a deep inspection of the condition of our soul.

Repentance is an essential component to forgiveness. What is repentance though? Tommy Tenney calls authentic repentance "an awesome flesh-death sight to behold." In our culture, repentance has lost its meaning and has been reduced to a simple, "Oops, God, I messed up again. Sorry about that." True repentance, however, is a gut-wrenching, soul-bearing, heartfelt grief over what we have done or failed to do. Because repentance is so grueling, why in the world would anyone want to put him or herself through this kind of agony?

To put it plainly, we do it so we might be forgiven. If we are willing to face the music and admit the wretched condition of our soul apart from God, confess our sin and throw ourselves at the mercy of the Court of Heaven, and turn from our evil ways, we will experience God's complete, unbelievable, wipe-the-slate-clean forgiveness.

"Repentance is not a fatal day when tears are shed, but a natal day when, as a result of tears, a new life begins."
—Ilion T. Jones

"To do so no more is the truest repentance."
—Martin Luther

"God will take nine steps toward us, but he will not take the tenth. He will incline us to repent, but he cannot do our repenting for us."
—A.W. Tozer

"Repent, then, and turn to God, so that your sins may be wiped out, that times of refreshing may come from the Lord."
—Acts 3:19

‹ 5 ›

Receive Christ as the Lord and Savior of your life.

"Have you ever tried shrimp?" they asked me. I gazed at a pile of what looked to be multi-legged, mummified, embryonic aliens. Despite their repulsive appearance and against my better judgment, I took a nibble, then another, then another. I proceeded to scarf down the entire plate of what I now consider to be delectable crustaceans. Much to my dismay, half an hour later my body was completely covered in large, red, itchy bumps. Although I thought I was stunningly handsome in large, red, itchy bumps, my parents became concerned. They rushed me to the emergency room, where I received some Benedryl and, thankfully, was soon back to normal (insert your own joke here).

Three years later, someone else asked me if I wanted a bite of shrimp. I partook (proving conclusively that inside my brain, the wheel is spinning but the hamster's dead). Thirty minutes later, and right on cue, I turned to our dinner guests and said, "I thwink ba thongue isth thwelling upth." (Translation: "I think my tongue is swelling up.") The next thing I knew, my throat began to inflate, and I started to have great difficulty breathing. Without fully grasping the consequences of my actions, I had done something very foolish and soon found myself in a fight for my life. Another frantic visit to the hospital and another lifesaving shot, and I was back to stupid, I mean normal.

Here's the question: What actually saved me? Was it the fact that I was now extremely conscious of the stupidity of my actions and deeply remorseful for doing them? Was it the mere knowledge that I desperately needed medicine? Was it that I truly believed in the healing attributes of Benedryl? No. Although these revelations led me to a necessary point of decision, it wasn't until I actually received the medicine that the healing began. As John 1:12 tells us, "Yet to all who received him, to those who believed in his name, he gave the right to become children of God." When we recognize that Christ died for our sins and that only God can save us, and when we invite Jesus into our hearts, then we become a child of God.

"Almost persuaded to be a Christian is like the man who was almost pardoned, but he was hanged, like the man who was almost rescued, but he was burned in the house. A man that is almost saved is damned."

—Charles Haddon Spurgeon

"There are too many grandchildren of Christ in the world, those whose parents were Christians, but they aren't. Nowhere in the Bible does God claim grandchildren—just children, born again by faith in Christ."

—Bob Pierce

I recently returned from a trip to the West. As I attempted to board the plane, the flight attendant asked for my ticket. She didn't ask about my occupation. She didn't ask how much money I had in my portfolio. She didn't ask if I was popular or athletic. She didn't ask where I was born, who my parents were, or to whom I was married. She simply asked for my airline ticket. If I had the ticket, I was able to board the plane and travel to my destination. Without the ticket, I was stranded. The non-ticket-related qualities about me were completely unimportant to her. My entire hope for traveling on that plane rested on my having or not having the ticket.

Similarly, one day we will all stand before God. At that time, He will not inquire about our investments, our ascent up the corporate ladder, our athletic achievements, our lineage, our popularity, or the like. I believe He will ask us each one question and one question alone: "Did you have a personal relationship with my Son, Jesus Christ, and receive Him as your personal Lord and Savior?"

In other words, Jesus is the ticket to heaven. Don't get me wrong, Jesus is waaayyy more than "fire insurance," but the fact of the matter is that our coming to God and our entry into paradise rests solely and completely on whether or not we possess the "ticket" God has so amazingly and generously provided. Jesus made no bones about this when He declared in John 14:6, *"I am the way and the truth and the life. No one comes to the Father except through me."*

"A person may go to heaven without health, without riches, without honors, without learning, without friends; but he can never go there without Christ."
—John Dyer

In this prologue, we have presented God's plan for your salvation. It calls for a decision that is yours and yours alone. No one can make this choice for you, and neither can it be avoided. To not decide for Christ is to decide against Him. Not to invite Christ into your heart is to shut Him out of your heart. If you have never asked Christ to be your Lord and Savior, or are unsure of your salvation, or if you would like to have a new beginning and rededicate your life to Christ, we invite you to pray this prayer sincerely from your heart:

Prayer to Receive Christ

Thank you, God, for loving me so much
that you sent your Son, Jesus Christ,
to die for my sins. I repent of my sins,
and I ask for your forgiveness
to make me clean in your sight.
I now receive Jesus Christ
as my personal Lord and Savior.
I give my life to you, and
I receive your eternal life.
Thank you for hearing my prayer
and for forgiving my sin.
In Jesus, name, amen.

If you just received Jesus, congratulations! You are now a new creation (2 Corinthians 5:17).

"Your sins are forgiven.
Your guilt is atoned for.
Your past is removed.
Your future is secured.
You have a peace in your heart.
You have a purpose to your step.
You have a song on your lips.
You are saved from hell.
You are right with God.
You are going to heaven."

—Anne Graham Lotz

Also, if you just received Jesus, tell a Christian friend and your pastor. This is the most important decision you will ever make, and we invite you to record this date on the next page. Your acceptance of Christ is not the end but the beginning of your journey with your new Lord and Savior. You're going to need fuel for the journey, and that's where the rest of this book comes in....

I, _____ , received

Christ on _____ , 20____ .

What Does It Mean to Be a Christian?

day one >>> **conversion**
day two >>> **purpose**

section

s e c t i o n

1

d a y 1 > > >

The Case of the Ethiopian Eunuch

(A "Who Dunnit" Mystery Theatre)

"Conversion is so simple that the smallest child can be converted, but it is also so profound that theologians throughout history have pondered the depth of its meaning."

—Billy Graham

It was a quiet day at the detective agency of Spade, Marlow, Magnum, Bogart, Murder She Wrote, and Columbo. My name is Percible Ignatius, but my clients call me P.I. I'm a private investigator.

Business was so slow I thought of closing up shop for a few days and taking a well-deserved vacation. All that changed with a knock at the door. She walked into my office and my life. In all my years in the business, I'd never seen anything like her. Kitty Carlyle was her name. She was a red-headed, blonde bombshell with luscious brown hair and a smile that could make a skydiver forget his parachute. I wanted to kiss her with every lip on my face. Instead, I inquired suavely,

"Well, dollface, how can I help you?"

Tears welled up in her deep green eyes and her pouting lips quivered as she informed me, "Something strange has happened to my brother."

Her voice was as sultry as a...as a...as a...well, let's just say it was really sultry. Finally, she spilled the beans.

"Don't worry," I said. "The cleaning lady will take care of those beans. Just tell me about your brother."

She began to unfurl the saga of her sibling's bizarre transformation. Her brother, an Ethiopian eunuch, was acting peculiar, and she was hoping that I could get to the bottom of it. I gazed into her sky-blue eyes and whispered romantically, "My rate is $10 a day, plus expenses."

"Consider yourself hired," she said in a voice that could make a bishop kick out a stained glass window. "But I feel it is only fair to warn you that there might be more to this mystery than just my brother."

"What do you mean?" I inquired, as her big brown eyes hypnotized me.

She went on to explain how several other people, including a blind man and a female cloth entrepreneur, all who had their lives inexplicably transformed. The case was becoming more complicated by the moment. What had happened? I had to find some answers, but it was becoming apparent that this case was too big to handle alone. I informed her that this new information would force me to bring on additional muscle.

"Do whatever it takes. I need to know the truth."

As this brunette beauty turned on her heels and left my office, her parting words echoed in my ears. "I must know the truth," she said.

That's my story, and I'm asking for your help. So slip on your hat and trench coat, grab your magnifying glass, and you be the detective. Something happened to these people. Using only your Bible and your wits, let's solve the puzzle by figuring out what revolutionized their lives forever.

"Here's looking at you kid."

FUEL

With your detective hat on, read these three conversion stories: Acts 8:26–38, Acts 9:1–19, and Acts 16:12–15/Acts 16:25–34.

‹ 1 ›

"Now an angel of the Lord said to Philip, 'Go south to the road—the desert road—that goes down from Jerusalem to Gaza.' So he started out, and on his way he met an Ethiopian eunuch, an important official in charge of all the treasury of Candace, queen of the Ethiopians. This man had gone to

Jerusalem to worship, and on his way home was sitting in his chariot reading the book of Isaiah the prophet. The Spirit told Philip, 'Go to that chariot and stay near it.' Then Philip ran up to the chariot and heard the man reading Isaiah the prophet. 'Do you understand what you are reading?' Philip asked. 'How can I,' he said, 'unless someone explains it to me?' So he invited Philip to come up and sit with him. The eunuch was reading this passage of scripture:

> 'He was led like a sheep to the slaughter, and as a lamb before the shearer is silent so he did not open his mouth. In his humiliation he was deprived of justice. Who can speak of his descendants? For his life was taken from the earth.'

The eunuch asked Philip, 'Tell me, please, who is the prophet talking about, himself or someone else?' Then Philip began with that very passage of scripture and told him the good news about Jesus. As they traveled along the road, they came to some water and the eunuch said, 'Look, here is water. Why shouldn't I be baptized?' And he gave orders to stop the chariot. Then both Philip and the eunuch went down into the water and Philip baptized him."

—Acts 8:26–38

‹ 2 ›

"Meanwhile, Saul was still breathing out murderous threats against the Lord's disciples. He went to the high priest and asked him for letters to the synagogues in Damascus, so that if he found any there who belonged to the Way, whether men or women, he might take them as prisoners to Jerusalem. As he neared Damascus on his journey, suddenly a light from heaven flashed around him. He fell to the ground and heard a voice say to him, 'Saul, Saul, why do you persecute me?' 'Who are you, Lord?' Saul asked. 'I am Jesus, whom you are persecuting,' He replied. 'Now get up and go into the city, and you will be told what you must do.' The men traveling with Saul stood there speechless; they heard the sound but did not see anyone. Saul got up from the ground, but when he opened his eyes he could see nothing. So they led him by the hand into Damascus."

—Acts 9:1–8

‹ 3 ›

"From there we traveled to Philippi, a Roman colony and the leading city of that district of Macedonia. And we stayed there several days. On the

Sabbath we went outside the city gate to the river, where we expected to find a place of prayer. We sat down and began to speak to the women who had gathered there. One of those listening was a woman named Lydia, a dealer in purple cloth from the city of Thyatira, who was a worshiper of God. The Lord opened her heart to respond to Paul's message. When she and the members of her household were baptized, she invited us to her home. 'If you consider me a believer in the Lord,' she said, 'come and stay at my house.' And she persuaded us."   —Acts 16:12–15

"Conversion simply means turning around."   —Vincent McNabb

You have just read the stories of three lives that were forever changed by Christ. In light of these conversions, we invite you to reflect on how you came to faith in Christ.

re**ACTION**

■ What do the conversions of the Ethiopian, Paul, and Lydia have in common? What is unique about each one?

■ What is different or unique about your own story?

■ What positive effect did Lydia's conversion have on her family?

■ What effect has your conversion had on your family?

■ As you read the remainder of the New Testament, you will discover that Paul's life became more difficult and more blessed by his encounter with Christ. How has your life become more wonderful and more challenging since receiving Jesus?

■ Is your conversion experience more like the Ethiopian's, Saul/Paul's, or Lydia's? How? Why?

■ Do you think these people considered their conversion as the end of their spiritual quest or the beginning of a spiritual journey?

"Conversion may occur in an instant, but the process of coming from sinful into a new life can be a long and arduous journey."

—Chuck Colson

If you have not yet been baptized, talk to your pastor about this important step in your faith.

day 2 > > >

Enemy Pantyhose

"So then, just as you received Christ Jesus as Lord, continue to live in him, rooted and built up in him, strengthened in the faith as you were taught, and overflowing with thankfulness." —Colossians 2:6–7

"Christianity has not been tried and found wanting...Christianity has been found difficult and, therefore, left untried." —G.K. Chesterton

It was the first time I had ever worn pantyhose on my head (or anywhere else for that matter). The game was called "Hosehead." The name is derived from the participants wearing pantyhose on top of their noggins. Let it be known that the contestants are not wearing hose on their heads as a deranged fashion statement or because they are anatomically confused. Instead, the captured hose indicates when the players are "caught," in the same way flags are used in flag football.

The object of this contest is to capture the other team's flag and bring it safely across the neutral, imaginary line separating the two teams. However, while you are endeavoring to acquire the opposition's flag, a regiment of enemy players is attempting to yank the pantyhose off the top of your head. Words cannot describe the experience of racing down a mountain at breakneck speed only to have someone wrench the pantyhose off your biological hat-rack, thereby practically separating your head from your shoulders. Such an experience gives a whole new meaning to having a run in your hose.

Anyway, if you have been "hosed," you must go to jail, where you are to remain until someone from your team brings you an enemy's pantyhose. Capturing an adversary's nylons is difficult enough. Freeing a captured combatant is even more challenging because the opponents always have Green Beret-type guards surrounding their prison to ensure that no breakout occurs.

During one memorable game, the opposing team (through cheating, corruption, and illegal steroid use) had managed to capture many of our players. Let me assure you that seeing the pitiful sight of your hoseless teammates begging you to rescue them will moisten the eyes of even the toughest combatant. Fortunately, my team (through our honest play, hard work, and legal use of caffeine) had our own plentiful collection of enemy hostages and pantyhose.

In our caffeine-infused bravado, we concocted a rescue strategy that seemed foolproof at the time. While my teammates created a diversion, I would attempt to deliver the cranial support hose to our imprisoned amigos. Our "diversion," henceforth known in military circles as "Stupid Plan A," failed miserably, and I was left as exposed as a bacon-wrapped Hobbit at an Orc's barbeque.

As I sprinted to deliver the goods, I suddenly found myself face-to-face with a thousand, perhaps a million (or at least six), enemy guards who were apparently working through some deep aggression issues. These now-salivating storm troopers immediately made me the target of years of apparent pent-up hostility. They were no match, however, for "Scared Half to Death Boy." With adrenaline coursing through my body (it wasn't the only thing that nearly went coursing through my body), I juked left, cut right, and left my would-be assailants in a humiliating cloud of dust as I passed the pantyhose to my awaiting teammates. No applause necessary. Oh, go ahead, if you must. Thank you.

Most of my freed team members exploded out of the jail with a triumphant shout and raced up the opponent's mountain, eager to defeat the enemy. Two guys, however, just stood at the base of the mountain like two inebriated sloths. Caught up in my recent act of heroism, a righteous indignation welled up within me. I wanted to shout to them, "Hey, you intoxicated, lethargic, tree mammals, I didn't risk my neck and set you free so you could sit around twiddling your thumbs! I set you free so we could complete our mission and capture the enemy's flag!"

In the same way, Jesus didn't set us free from sin and death to sit on our blessed assurances and lollygag through life until He finally takes us home. If all there is to the Christian life is making it to heaven, then Jesus would send us there as soon as we receive His salvation. The fact that you and I are still on this earth tells us that we have a job to do.

> We have friends to reach,
> the hungry to feed,
> prayers to pray,
> Christians to encourage,
> the sick to care for,
> the imprisoned to visit,
> evil to confront,
> captives to set free,
> ministries to support,
> forgiveness to proclaim,
> hope to offer,
> love to demonstrate,
> and a mission to fulfill.

Ephesians 2:10 informs us that *"we are God's workmanship, created in Christ Jesus to do good works, which God prepared in advance for us to do."* In addition, Colossians 2:6–7 tells us that *"...just as you received Christ Jesus as Lord, continue to live in Him, rooted and built up in Him, strengthened in the faith as you were taught, and overflowing with thankfulness."* In other words, you and I were designed for a destiny, produced for a purpose, and blessed in order that we might be a blessing to others.

"Discipleship and salvation are two different things: A disciple is one who, realizing the meaning of the atonement, deliberately gives himself up to Jesus Christ in unspeakable gratitude." —Oswald Chambers

---

I like Rick Warren's analogy of comparing the Christian life to a base-ball field. In this model, *knowing Christ* is represented by first base. According to the rules of baseball, if you don't touch first base, you will never get "home." In the same way, coming to know Christ in a personal way is absolutely vital to the Christian life. While getting on base is crucial in baseball, there is much more to the game than simply making it to first base. The object is to get players around the bases in order to score runs. Likewise, we must understand that coming into a personal relationship with Jesus isn't the end of the Christian life. Instead, it is only a wonderful beginning.

Second base represents *growing in Christ*. As parents, we don't want our children to stay infants forever. Instead, we want them to grow and mature. In fact, if they *don't*, it's a sign that something is very wrong. In the same way, not only does Jesus desire for us to become adopted into His family, He also wants us to grow and mature in the faith. If we're not growing in our knowledge of and our relationship with Christ, it's a sign that something is amiss.

Third base means we are *serving Christ*. God wants us to get out of the pew and make a difference in the world. Not long ago, a promotion at a major league baseball stadium issued a free ticket to any child who brought a baseball mitt to the game. When the ticket counter asked a little girl where her glove was, she exclaimed, "I just came to watch, I didn't know I was going to get to play!"

Likewise, many people view salvation as nothing more than a free ticket to heaven. However, it is so important that we understand that Jesus never gave us a mitt so that we might sit in the bleachers. Instead, we have each been picked to play on the team.

"Christ died for me. What am I doing for him?" —Anonymous

Home plate is all about *sharing Christ*. Amazingly, here is how it has worked for the last 2,000 years: Andrew told Peter, Peter told Cornelius, Cornelius told someone, and two millenniums later, someone told you. Somebody cared enough to inform you that God loves you and sent His Son who died on a cross that you might have new life. Who are you going to tell?

In conclusion, God's desire for our lives runs deeper than praying a prayer to receive Him. He wants us to become fully-devoted followers who are growing in Christ, serving Christ, and sharing Christ. Welcome to the Big Leagues. Run the bases well, and don't forget your pantyhose.

"The world has yet to see what God can do with and for and through and in a man who is fully and wholly consecrated to Christ."

—Henry Varley

"Grow in grace and knowledge of our Lord Jesus Christ."

—II Peter 3:18

"Let us leave the elementary teachings about Christ and go on to maturity."

—Hebrews 6:1

re ACTION

Did you come to watch or to play? Where do you find yourself in the baseball diamond analogy?

1) *Stuck in a squeeze play between first and second:*
   Where do you most need to grow as a Christian?

   ❏ Prayer.
   ❏ Holiness of living.
   ❏ Forgiveness.
   ❏ Witnessing.
   ❏ Fasting.
   ❏ Scripture memory.
   ❏ Personal Bible study.
   ❏ Group Bible study.
   ❏ Worship.
   ❏ Outreach.

2) *Rounding second and beginning to serve Christ:*
Check and answer the question below that best fits what might be God's purpose for your life today.

- ❑ Could you skip lunch and give the money to a hunger relief organization in your community?
- ❑ Which ministry at church could you serve?
- ❑ Is there a lawn you could mow, a cake you could bake, or a visit you could make to an elderly person in your community?
- ❑ To whom in your family could you show kindness, understanding, and love? Who do you know who needs a listening ear?
- ❑ Is there someone in the hospital you could visit?
- ❑ Is there a family member or a friend in prison to whom you could write a letter?
- ❑ Could you send a letter of encouragement to a missionary? (Your pastor can probably give you the name and address of a missionary your church supports.)
- ❑ Is there a short-term mission trip you could go on?

3) *Headed for home plate:*
Who could you befriend today at school or work?

What friend could you witness to today?

Reaching Up: Growing in Our Relationship with God

FUE

section

2

d a y 3 › › ›

No Strings Attached

"*When we have not met God in the center of our hearts, we cannot expect to meet Him in the business of our lives.*" —John Chrysostom

Brace yourself: I am about to impart to you some really, really deep theology: Faith is like getting a free guitar. Stop laughing at me. No, really, your relationship to Christ is like the story of how I got my guitar. Here's the story: I mentioned to a friend of mine (For the last time I told you to stop laughing—I do have friends.)...If I may start again? I mentioned to a friend of mine that I would like to learn to play the guitar. A couple of days later he showed up at my door with a new Yamaha acoustic in his hand. He handed it to me, a free gift, no strings attached. Okay, the guitar had strings, but the gift didn't. (Now you can laugh.) He simply said, "Learn to play."

Now I want you to ask me if I can play. Go ahead, ask. No, I cannot, but thanks for rubbing it in. I tried twice, but I haven't plucked a note since. Again, I say your relationship to Christ is like my receiving this guitar. E. Stanley Jones once said, "Knowing Christ is the act of a moment and the work of a lifetime." This relationship is a gift we receive, but it takes intentional time and effort for that gift to blossom.

Once that gift is received, every believer needs to make four disciplines an integral part of his or her life. **Jesus exemplified these four amazingly beneficial habits:**

Amazingly Beneficial Habit ‹ 1 ›
B I B L E   S T U D Y

Mark Twain said, "A man who can read good books and doesn't, is no better off than a man who can't read." Likewise, a person who believes that the Bible is vital to their faith, yet doesn't study it, is no better off than a person who doesn't even possess a Bible. The only Bible we truly own is not the one we hold in our hands, but the one we hold in our hearts. If you earnestly desire to draw closer to Christ, decide right now to make nourishing your soul through Bible study as important and routine as nourishing your body with food.

"A Bible that's falling apart probably belongs to someone who isn't."

—Christian Johnson

"The family Bible is more often used to adorn coffee tables or press flowers than it is to feed souls and discipline lives."

—Charles Colson

Amazingly Beneficial Habit ‹ 2 ›
P R A Y E R

In today's society, our calendars, day planners, and palm pilots are jam-packed with activity. Because of this frantic pace, our lives could be compared to a backyard kickball game in which prayer is, unfortunately, the last activity chosen and the first one cut from the team.

This was not the case with Christ. If Jesus had a Day-Timer, you could rest assured that he would have penciled in time for prayer on every page. That is especially amazing when you consider that no one had a more important task or more pressing needs than Christ. Despite these pressing demands on Jesus' time and attention, the Bible tells us that it was His custom to find solitude in order to communicate with His Heavenly Father.

I live in a small town. One morning I ran into my friend Jerry who was eating breakfast at a restaurant. I saw him again that afternoon in the grocery store. Later that evening, I looked up from my cheeseburger at McDonald's, and there was Jerry's smiling face. (I go out to eat a lot, but that's not the point.) In the same way, if you meet Christ in your heart in prayer, I bet you'll run into Him all day long.

Amazingly, at any time of the day, God greatly desires to talk to you. Have you ever considered the awesome fact that the God of the universe has a passion to converse with you? Chew on this awhile: If God had a refrigerator, your picture would be on it. If God had a bicep, your face would be tattooed on it. If He had a wallet, your photo would be in it. He loves you and desires an intimate relationship with you. Amazing, isn't it? So find a quiet place where you can pray and seek His face. Tell Him your heart's desires. Tell Him where it hurts.

"God does nothing except in answer to prayers." — John Wesley

---

Amazingly Beneficial Habit ‹ 3 ›
FELLOWSHIP WITH OTHER CHRISTIANS

Jesus had a habit of getting together with a handful of folks to dig deeper into what it means to follow the Father. Jesus often had the disciples withdraw from the crowds for times of teaching and prayer. Likewise, at the garden of Gethsemane, Jesus desperately desired to have His friends wrestle with Him in prayer. If the Son of God believed it vital to be part of a small group of committed followers, how can we have the audacity to think that we can fly solo? In other words, we need each other. Find a small group of Christians with whom you can meet regularly to pray, study, hold each other accountable, and encourage each other in your faith. If there's nothing like that in your church or school, then take the bull by the horns and start something. Don't skip this one. Determine to find a small group with whom you can open up your heart, let down your hair, and take off your mask.

"The Bible knows nothing of a solitary religion." —John Wesley

"An arch consists of two weaknesses, which leaning against one another make a strength." —Leonardo da Vinci

Amazingly Beneficial Habit < 4 >
MINISTRY

Jesus helped people everywhere He went, and He wants us to do the same. God has something wonderful He wants you to do. Ephesians 2:10 tells us *"For we are God's workmanship, created in Christ Jesus to do good works, which God prepared in advance for us to do."* In other words, you were created and saved for a purpose: to serve. I bet you already know a hurting person you can help or a ministry in your church you can plug into and make a difference.

"I try to give to the poor people for love what the rich could get for money. No, I wouldn't touch a leper for a thousand pounds; yet I willingly cure him for the love of God." —Mother Teresa

These four disciplines of scripture, prayer, discipleship, and ministry are irreplaceable and indispensable. They are like the four legs of a chair. If one is missing, you'll have a three-legged chair, which means your life will be out of balance.

FUEL

1) **SCRIPTURE:** *"He went into the synagogue as was his custom."*

—Luke 4:16

2) **PRAYER:** *"But Jesus often withdrew to lonely places and prayed."*

—Luke 5:16

3) **DISCIPLESHIP:** *"He taught them again as was his custom."*

—Mark 10:1

4) **MINISTRY:** *"He went around doing good."*   —Acts 10:38

reACTION

■ Which of the above spiritual habits do you find easier?

■ Which one(s) do you most struggle to fulfill?

■ What are two things you can do, starting today, to strengthen those weak areas?

1)

2)

"Faith is not a pill you take, it's a muscle you use."   —A.W. Tozer

day 4 › › ›

Bible Studies for Dummies

> *"Ignorance of Scripture is ignorance of Christ."*
> —St. Jerome

> *"In all my perplexities and distresses, the Bible has never failed to give me light and strength."*
> —Robert E. Lee

> *"I am sorry for men who do not read the Bible every day. I wonder why they deprive themselves of the strength and the pleasure."*
> —Woodrow Wilson

Congratulations on purchasing the Ran-Co E-600 3.2 Deluxe Scripture Study—Student Edition 7.4. *WARNING! Before opening your Bible, please thoroughly review the instruction manual after verifying that the following inventory is included in your package:*

- 47 translations of the Bible for comparison (heretofore referred to as 47TOTBFC)
- *Strong's Bible Concordance*, *Weak's Bible Dictionary*, *Wimpy's Theological Encyclopedia*, and *Comatose's Greek and Hebrew Lexicon*

- *The Romulian Vulgate Pseudepigrapha Parchments* (Revised Edition)
- Yohan Berskendorf's *Condensed History of the Christian Church Volume 1–223*
- *Karl Barth's Cross-Stitching and the Minor Prophets*

We have made every effort to ensure that all parts are included. If, however, something is missing, please call us toll free at 1-800-CONFUSED to request a replacement part. Allow six weeks to three generations for delivery. Tax and title not included. Void where prohibited. Parents, get your children's permission before calling. Member FDIC. Illinois residents need not apply.

You are now almost ready to begin. First, open your 47TOTBFC Bible. Please refer to diagram one, section A, paragraph II, line seven. Placing your left foot on the USB Port, plug parallel B (marked as parallel C7) into your right digital flux capacitor, next yadda, blah blah blah...

The above instructions would intimidate the begeebers out of anyone. Most people never read their Bible because they fear it will be worse than following the instructions to program a DVD player.

More than 500 years, ago Martin Luther's barber, who was a new believer, asked Luther for a straightforward and simple way to begin to study the Bible. The barber gave him a bad haircut, and Luther gave his barber some great advice. (Seriously, I've seen a sketch of Martin Luther and it looks like the guy used a Ran-Co combination Weed Whacker and Salad Shooter on Luther's head). "Bad Hair Day" Martin told his friend to approach a particular Bible passage as if it were a rope with four strands. Using this method, Luther and his hair samurai studied the Ten Commandments together.

"Out of each commandment I make a [rope] of four twisted strands. That is, I take each commandment first as a <u>teaching</u>, which is what it actually is, and I reflect upon what our Lord God so earnestly requires of me here. Secondly, I make out of it a <u>reason for thanksgiving</u>. Thirdly, a <u>confession</u> and fourthly, a <u>prayer petition</u>."

—Martin Luther

Tackle the text below using "Chia Head" Luther's method. Look at each strand individually, and then put them all together to make the rope (and text) complete:

> *"If you have any encouragement from being united with Christ, if any comfort from his love, if any fellowship with Spirit, if any tenderness and compassion, then make my joy complete by being likeminded, having the same love, being one in spirit and purpose. Do nothing out of selfish ambition or vain conceit, but in humility consider others better than yourselves. Each of you should look not only to your own interests, but also to the interest of others. Your attitude should be the same as that of Christ Jesus"* (Philippians 2:1–5).

Strand One: T E A C H I N G

■ What do the above verses from Philippians teach you?

   ■ About yourself:

   ■ About Christ:

   ■ About relationships:

   ■ About life, money, sex, work, etc. (pick one):

"The Bible was not given to increase our knowledge. It was given to change lives."

                                  —D.L. Moody

Strand Two: T H A N K S G I V I N G

■ Re-read the Philippian passage. What does it make you grateful for?

■ Who in your life exemplifies the humility, tenderness, or compassion the text speaks about?

"A single line in the Bible has consoled me more than all the books I have ever read."
—Immanuel Kant

Strand Three: C O N F E S S I O N

■ Read the passage again with this question in mind: In light of these verses, what needs changing in your life?

Strand Four: P R A Y E R   P E T I T I O N

■ Who or what does this passage remind you to pray for (something that you would not have prayed for before you read it)?

"A man who loves his wife will love her letters and her photographs because they speak to him of her. So if we love the Lord Jesus, we shall love the Bible because it speaks to us of him." — John R. W. Stott

"All Scripture is God-breathed and useful for teaching, rebuking, correcting, and training in righteousness, so the man of God may be thoroughly equipped for every good work." —2 Timothy 3:16

"Thank You, Lord that my hair does not look like Martin Luther's..."

no, really...

"Open Your Word to me that it might change my life..."

day 5 › › ›

A Person Without Prayer

"A man without prayer is like a tree without roots."

—Pope Pius XII

"A person without prayer is like soap on a rope, without the soap, or the rope."

—Andy and Lowell

"A person without prayer is like a prayerless person."

—Lowell and Andy

"Lord, teach us to pray."

—The Disciples

Leonard Ravenhill said, "Prayer is profoundly simple and simply profound." When you get right down to it, prayer is extremely easy. It is simply talking with the God who loves you and desires to know you. He is more eager to hear your prayers and answer those prayers than you are to pray. However, as Yogi Berra never said, "While prayer is easy, it sure ain't simple." Prayer is somewhat like swimming in the ocean: The more you dive into it, the more incredible it becomes. In a hundred lifetimes, you could never fully explore its vast beauty and depth.

"To pray is to change. As Christians, we will either allow prayer to change and grow us in the image of Christ, or we will stop praying."

—Richard Foster

Below is a Biblical model for prayer to help you cover the basics and stay on track as you pray. So let us P-R-A-Y:

P R A I S E

Begin by praising God for who He is, for what He has done, and for what He is doing in your life. Thank Him for answered prayer and for all the incredible blessings you enjoy. Praise Him for His attributes, His love, His faithfulness, and His mercy. Don't rush through this part. Seek His heart before you seek His hand.

"Prayer is not a technique, it is a falling in love." —Richard Foster

R E P E N T

In the original language, "repent" literally means, "change your mind." We need to start thinking the way God does. We are sorry for our thoughts, words, and deeds because they have hurt the heart of God. Most likely, we hurt other people in some way as well. Repentance, however, is more than just feeling bad about what we've said or done—it implies that we change our direction. In other words, we are heading one way and make a U-turn and start heading a different direction. Repentance involves changing the way we think, feel, and act.

Repentance in prayer involves confessing to God what we have done. Be as specific as possible here. Don't just ask God to forgive you of all your sins and then go on. Tell Him exactly what you've done. By the way, you aren't telling God anything He doesn't already know; it's just that until we own up to our sins, we can't disown them. Then we ask for and receive His forgiveness. When we do this, God gives us the wonderful promise that *"If we confess our sins, He is faithful and just to forgive our sins and purify* us from all unrighteousness" (I John 1:9). Even if you don't yet *feel* forgiven, when you are truly sorry and desire to live a different life, trust God that you *are* forgiven.

"A sinful man will stop praying, and a praying man will stop sinning."

—Leonard Ravenhill

ASK

Pray for others. Make a list of people who are dear to your heart. Pray specifically for their needs. Risk. Step out in faith. Pray boldly. Pray for the hurting, the hungry, the sick, and the persecuted. Pray for the lost, the lonely, and the brokenhearted. Ask God to soften your heart toward the needs of others. Pray for your pastor, youth leaders, teachers, co-workers, and missionaries. Don't forget to pray for national and world leaders.

As fallen, sinful human beings, we are naturally self-centered. We tend to focus on our own problems. Praying for others gives the Holy Spirit permission to break these chains of selfishness.

Now here's the hard part: Pray for people you may not like or people who get on your nerves. Pray even for those you hold grudges against. (Deal with that grudge in the repentance part of prayer as well.) Although it's not easy, the Bible is clear that we are to pray for our enemies (Matthew 5:44). These prayers make room for the Holy Spirit to change our attitude, setting us free from the prison of bitterness and anger.

Finally, begin to look expectantly throughout the day for the ways God is answering your prayers, and thank Him for those answers.

"Pray for each other..."

—James 5:16

YOURSELF

While God is not a cosmic genie or vending machine that exists for our pleasure and whims, He is a loving Heavenly Father who is thrilled to meet the needs and answer the prayers of His children. Jesus invites us to ask Him for things (Matthew 7:7). Likewise, James 4:2 informs us that we *"do not have because we do not ask God,"* but he also goes on to tell us that motive is important. If it matters to you, it matters to God, so don't be afraid to come to Him with your concerns.

"The shortest distance between a problem and a solution is the distance between your knees and the floor. The one who kneels to the Lord can stand up to anything." —Author Unknown

FUEL

"If you, then, though you are evil, know how to give good gifts to your children, how much more will your Father in heaven give good gifts to those who ask Him." —Matthew 7:11

P R A I S E : _____

_____

_____

R E P E N T : _____

_____

_____

A S K for others: _____

_____

_____

Pray for Y O U R S E L F : _____

_____

_____

"As it is the business of tailors to make clothes and of cobblers to mend shoes, so it is the business of Christians to pray." —Martin Luther

day 6 > > >

Quivering Doughnuts

> *"Worship is not a part of the Christian life; it is the Christian life."*
>
> —Gerald Vann

> *"If worship does not change us, it has not been worship. To stand before the Holy One of eternity is to change. Worship begins in holy expectancy; it ends in holy obedience."*
>
> —Richard J. Foster

> *"Worship is giving to God the best he has given us."*
>
> —Oswald Chambers

To this day, the memory of the impromptu doughnut-eating contest that occurred prior to one of our youth group meetings still brings a smile to my face. Tim, the reigning, undefeated champion of past contests (which included Vienna sausages, marshmallows, and hot dogs) was an eating machine. Raymond, his opponent, was no slouch either. Although Raymond had never eaten professionally, he was a ranking contender among amateurs, competing in the grueling "11th Plague" division.

Even though Tim was a six-wiener-a-day hot dog junky, he had never consumed doughnuts in head-to-head competition. That's why local bookies had given Raymond a slight edge.

The two fierce warriors faced each other as they prepared for battle. Six dozen doughnuts shook in fear as they waited to be consumed in the black hole of male teenage hunger. The crowd roared. The bell rang. Okay, technically there were no bookies, the "crowd" consisted of just five other people, the "roar" that reverberated was likely just a belch of the Richter scale variety, and, to be honest, we had no bell. On the other hand, someone did actually bump the table causing the doughnuts to move, if not shake. Suddenly in a blur of hands, sugar, and deep-fried dough, the contest began. With little collateral damage (unless you count the "pinky finger incident"), the event was over in less than three minutes. In the end, only one bloated teen could leave victorious. When the powdered sugar had settled, Tim had once again emerged triumphant.

Before Tim could finish his "victory dance" (a flurry of gyrations that sent small, woodland creatures scurrying for cover and was deemed indecent in seven Midwestern states), our youth counselor entered the room, carrying all the fixings for a hot dog feast, which happened to be Tim's favorite meal. There are certain statements you think you'll never hear:

- Your little brother saying, "You can have the last piece of chocolate cake if you want."
- Your husband saying, "Here, honey, you take the remote for awhile."
- Your wife proclaiming, "With this purchase, I won't need to shop for clothes again this year!"
- A politician saying, "Actually, my opponent is a much better candidate than I am."

Just as those statements would stun their hearers, Tim announcing, "No thanks, I don't want any hot dogs" nearly sent our youth counselor into a state of shock.

"He is not going to pour out His Spirit where He doesn't find hunger."

—Tommy Tenney

Even the most scrumptious gourmet dinners, without hunger, remain uneaten. What is true of food is also true of worship. For worship to fill, empower, and transform us, we need to be hungry for God. Most of us have no control over what happens in our worship services on Sunday. We may not be able to make the guy beside us sing with gusto or wake the lady on the front row. But what we *can* do will strengthen our walk with Christ and may eventually affect the attitude of our whole church.

We can come to church *hungry* for God, thirsty to know Christ, yearning for strength to be faithful, expecting to hear His voice, gain His guidance, and experience His forgiveness. Worship is not just something you attend or do. Worship is the attitude and act of giving ourselves wholly to God, exalting His name, and yearning for and adoring Him.

"God wants worshipers before workers; indeed the only acceptable workers are those who have learned the lost art of worship."

—A.W. Tozer

Some Facts About Worship

W O R S H I P isn't limited to a particular place or time.

Quite often, we associate worship with a particular place (church) at a particular time (Sunday morning). While the Bible clearly mandates that we join together regularly in public worship (Hebrews 10:25), that isn't the only place where worship can occur. The great news is that we can worship God any place and at any time. We can praise and worship the Lord while taking a shower, driving in our car, tucking our kids in bed at night, or taking a walk in a park. There is something far more vital than the location in regards to worship, and that is our attitude.

W O R S H I P demands our involvement.

At the first church I pastored, I quite often began the message with a humorous story. On one particular Sunday morning, I heard the congregation laughing much more generously than that particular joke deserved. I also noticed that instead of looking at me, all eyes were fixed on something happening behind me. I turned around only to discover that each of the choir members had a placard and had me rated anywhere from one to ten, a la diving or gymnastic competitions. While my choir's mischievous activity cracked us all up, the sad reality is that many people attend worship services with a "placard" attitude. They rate the music, rate the message, and rate the worship service overall. Those who approach worship in this way, however, have missed the whole point of worship. These people mistakenly view the preacher, the worship team, the choir, the soloist, and the like as the only ones involved in worship, and, at the same time, they mistakenly perceive themselves to be the audience. In true worship, however, we are all worshiping participants, and God is the only audience. In authentic worship, there is always an audience of One.

"To worship is
  to quicken the conscience by the holiness of God,
    to feed the mind with the truth of God,
      to purge the imagination by the beauty of God,
        to open the heart to the love of God,
          to devote the will to the purpose of God."
                                    —Archbishop William Temple

W O R S H I P is not limited by circumstances.

In Philippi, Paul and Silas were severely beaten, thrown into prison, and had their feet put in the stocks. But instead of sulking or fuming as one would expect people to do in such distressing conditions, we find them worshiping God. Their backs may have been bleeding, but their lips were praising. Likewise, God is just as worthy of praise when we are in the dungeons of life as He is when everything is peachy. And who knows, just as the chains fell off of Paul and Silas' feet and just as their prison doors flew open as they began to praise, God may set us free from some of our bondages and shackles as we worship Him.

W O R S H I P is not based on outward forms.

People worship God in different ways. Some prefer to worship in quietness and contemplation (*"Be still, and know that I am God."* —Psalm 46:10), while others are much more demonstrative (*"Clap your hands...shout to God with cries of joy. Lift up your hands in the sanctuary and praise the LORD"* —Psalm 47:1,134:2). Jesus, however, makes it clear that our outward form of expression isn't nearly as important as our inward attitude: *"Yet a time is coming and has now come when the true worshipers will worship the Father in spirit and truth, for they are the kind of worshipers the Father seeks. God is spirit, and his worshipers must worship in spirit and in truth"* (John 4:23–24). In other words, sincerity and passion are key. If a person's heart isn't genuine, whether that individual is sitting calmly in a pew or jumping the pew, all the person is doing is performing religious motions that never touch the heart of God.

"We have lost the art of adoring the Lord. Our worship gets so cluttered with endless strings of shallow and insincere words that all we do most of the time is 'take up time' or 'put in prayer time' with a passionless monologue that even God must ignore."

—Tommy Tenney

"Whatever is outward in worship must come as a direct result of what is inward—otherwise, it will be form without power."

—Howard Brinton

W O R S H I P demands our all.

If you have ever attended a major sporting event, you've probably witnessed worship. If you've ever seen the old clips of The Beatles concerts, you have an indication of what worship is all about. Worship engages our heart, soul, strength, and mind. It isn't based on emotions, but it certainly affects our emotions as well as our thoughts and actions. Worship is what caused David to do his "undignified" dance before the Ark of the Covenant (II Samuel 6:14,22), what inspired David and the Israelites to *"celebrate with all their might"* before God (I Chronicles 13:8), and what drove Ezekiel and John to fall prostrate before Him (Ezekiel 1:28, Revelation 1:17). In other words, these people were unable to be in the presence of God and remain unaffected, unlike many people today involved in our "worship" who appear to be baptized in lemon juice and weaned on a pickle. While I thoroughly enjoy a good game, it always amazes me how we can uninhibitedly demonstrate our adoration of our sports heroes or celebrities, who have never done more for our lives than momentarily entertain us, yet we appear to be impassionate in our worship of the King of Kings and Lord of Lords, who created us, who has given us all of our bountiful blessings, and who was willing to take our place on the cross.

"Worship is the highest and noblest act that any person can do. When men worship, God is satisfied! And when you worship, you are fulfilled! Think about this: why did Jesus Christ come? He came to make worshipers out of rebels." —Raymond C. Ortlund

Open your Bible to the very middle. Unless you have a boatload of maps and a concordance, you should find yourself in the book of Psalms—a book of praise and worship. Maybe the Lord was trying to tell us something when He put this book of praise in the middle of scripture. Just as the act of praise and worship is at the heart of His Word, so also should it be at the center of our lives and at the center of our relationship with Him.

"I will praise you, O LORD, with all my heart; I will tell of all your wonders. I will be glad and rejoice in you; I will sing praise to your name, O Most High." —Psalm 9:1–2

"The Lord says: 'These people come near to me with their mouth and honor me with their lips, but their hearts are far from me. Their worship of me is made up only of rules taught by men.'" —Isaiah 29:13

"David and all the Israelites were celebrating with all their might before God, with songs and with harps, lyres, tambourines, cymbals and trumpets."
—I Chronicles 13:8

"Praise the LORD. Praise God in his sanctuary; praise him in his mighty heavens. Praise him for his acts of power; praise him for his surpassing greatness. Praise him with the sounding of the trumpet, praise him with the harp and lyre, praise him with tambourine and dancing, praise him with the strings and flute, praise him with the clash of cymbals, praise him with resounding cymbals. Let everything that has breath praise the LORD. Praise the LORD." —Psalm 150

reACTION

This week, try TWO things you've never done before in your private and public worship. Here are a few options:

- ❏ During your prayer time, pick a favorite praise chorus or hymn to sing softly.
- ❏ Worship in the car. Sing embarrassingly loud!
- ❏ During your prayer time, choose a favorite Psalm or Bible passage and read it to God.
- ❏ Pray on your knees, humbling your heart to God.
- ❏ Lift your hands in worship.
- ❏ Visit a church that has a worship style that is dramatically different than your church.
- ❏ Give a testimony in your own church.
- ❏ Write a letter to God.
- ❏ Volunteer for a solo or duet in worship or contribute in other ways using the talents God gave you (playing an instrument, serving as a greeter, reading a Bible passage, etc.).
- ❏ Ask the pastor if your youth group can utilize drama during worship.
- ❏ Take notes during the sermon. Re-read those notes during the week. (And no, doodling on the bulletin does not count as taking notes.)

How faithful have you been in your worship attendance? Is there a mid-week, Sunday night, or contemporary service at your church? Show up! Show up hungry for God. Participate! Sing with passion and gusto.

Arrive fifteen minutes early to your church's next worship service in order to pray. Pray for your heart to be open and receptive to God. Pray for your pastor. Pray for a spiritual hunger in the other worshipers.

PRAYER starter

"God, give me a hunger for You..."

Reaching Over:
Growing in Our
Relationships with
Other Christians

day seven >>> **church**
day eight >>> **friendship**

s e c t i o n

FUEL

3

day 7 > > >

Rah, Rah, Rah, Sis Boom Bah!

"Be united with other Christians. A wall with loose bricks is not good. The bricks must be cemented together." —Corrie ten Boom

Cassie, a mild-mannered student at Run-of-the-Mill High School, is about to take "The Inquisition," a geometry exam so difficult that it requires a doctor's permission just to attempt. Side affects of this exam have included memory loss, hair loss, explosive acne, nausea, memory malfunction, simultaneous diarrhea and constipation, and loss of memory. Cassie is confident that she will fail "The Inquisition" and relatively certain that she is about to lose her breakfast. She is in the midst of a prayer concerning spontaneous combustion when, without warning, a pom-pom-bearing, perky-faced, cheerleading squad bursts into the room, surrounds Cassie's desk, and begins to chant,

"CASSIE, CASSIE, SHE'S OUR GIRL! DON'T
YOU WORRY, YOU WON'T HURL!
CASSIE, CASSIE, TURN IT LOOSE, AND
DETERMINE THE HYPOTENUSE!"

Wouldn't it be wonderful if every time you faced a difficult task, a group of spunky cheerleaders would begin to encourage you to greatness?

ENCOURAGEMENT

Have you ever wondered how the same basketball team that lost seventy percent of its games played on the road can somehow win seventy percent of its home games? At both locations they have the same coach, players, opponents, ball, and the same lousy refs, yet they often experience totally different results. The secret, of course, is that at home they enjoy the support of their fans. When playing at home the players are encouraged, applauded, challenged, and cheered to play their best, and they usually rise to the level of support they receive.

We also need that same kind of support as we grow in our faith. God has given us brothers and sisters in Christ to encourage us as Christians.

We are instructed to "...consider how we may spur one another on toward love and good deeds. Let us not give up meeting together, as some are in the habit of doing, but let us encourage one another...."

—Hebrews 10:24–25

In other words, God intends for the body of Christ to be a place where we experience the "home court advantage," no matter what the world throws our way. This world has a way of taking the wind out of our sails and throwing water on our fire, but God has given us the church so that we can challenge, cheer, and encourage each other in the game of life.

"I could go to the phone right now and call five friends who'd give me a car, a kidney, or take me into their home if I was in need. This is one of the greatest blessings of my life." —Bill Hybels

INSPIRATION

Not only does God intend for us to find encouragement in the family of God, He also wants us to experience inspiration as well. If you were to take some tongs and grab a coal from a barbecue and place that ember by itself, it would only be a matter of time until that coal would cool. It would gradually transform in color from white to red to pink to gray, and finally to black as the coal's heat diminished. On the other hand, if you took that same cold coal and placed it back with the other live coals, it would quickly reheat and turn white-hot again. In the same way, as we spend time around "on fire" Christians, it stokes our faith. Likewise, as we heat up, we will stoke the faith of our fellow brothers and sisters as well. Proverbs 27:17 tells us that, *"As iron sharpens iron, so one man sharpens another."* That means that as we fellowship with and inspire each other as growing Christians, everybody's faith is strengthened.

"How many people stop because so few say, 'Go!'"

—Charles R. Swindoll

PROTECTION

There is also protection in the body of Christ, the church. If you have ever watched the Discovery Channel, you have likely witnessed a once happy, isolated zebra transformed into a lion's McZebra Happy Meal. Just as there is safety in numbers on the African savanna, there is safety in numbers in the body of Christ.

"Two are better than one, because they have a good return for their work: If one falls down, his friend can help him up. But pity the man who falls and has no one to help him up! Also, if two lie down together, they will keep warm. But how can one keep warm alone? Though one may be overpowered, two can defend themselves. A cord of three strands is not quickly broken."

—Ecclesiastes 4:9–12

It is important to note that while the church is supposed to be this place of encouragement, inspiration, and protection, it sometimes fails to live up to its calling. You should remember these three extremely important principles when you pull into that building with the steeple, next to the graveyard:

1) The church is full of sinners, so of course it is going to mess up frequently and fall on its face occasionally. Hospitals are a place for the sick. Church is a place for sinners.

2) Jesus loves His church, warts and all. Jesus has used the fellowship of believers, despite its many failures, to be the greatest outreach of love this world has ever known. For 2,000 years, church has been a place where lives have changed, sinners have found forgiveness, orphans have found homes, the hungry have been fed, the sick have been healed, the hopeless have found hope, the helpless have found help, alcoholics have conquered addiction, children have learned to read, and marriages have been restored. Church, at its best, is where we find love when we don't deserve it, accountability when we fail, an extended family when we're lonely, and encouragement even when we've given up.

3) We don't just belong to the church—we *are* the church. Never forget that you're one of the sinners who causes the church to stumble. Its problems are your problems...so instead of pointing a finger, reach out a hand, because we're all in this together.

"We don't live alone. We are members of one body. We are responsible for each other. And I tell you that the time will soon come when, if men will not learn that lesson, then they will be taught it in fire and blood and anguish."

—J.B. Priestly

reACTION

■ Who has been a "cheerleader" for you in your walk with Christ? Take a moment to thank God for that person.

■ Who within your circle of friends or family needs some "cheering" up?

■ What "fires you up" most as a Christian?
- ❑ Worship.
- ❑ Spending time with other believers.
- ❑ Getting involved in ministry.
- ❑ A good message.
- ❑ A good concert.
- ❑ A good example.
- ❑ Digging in the Word with other believers.

■ Which best describes your faithfulness to the Body of Christ?
- ❑ Missing In Action (You only recognize the church inside with Christmas poinsettias, Easter lilies, a bride, or a coffin up front.)
- ❑ Army Reserve (You show up periodically.)
- ❑ Reluctant Draftee (Your posterior is in the pew, but your heart is A.W.O.L.)
- ❑ Front Line Fighter (While not a perfect soldier, you are in the battle and eager to please your commanding officer.)

■ Do you have any friends who are in danger of being lion chow because they are emotionally isolated or weak? What can you do to help bring them back in the fold?

day 8 > > >

Climbing Partners

"A real friend is one who helps us to think our noblest thoughts, to put forth our best efforts, and be our best selves." —Anonymous

I was fifteen years old and attending a Christian camp in Colorado. We were each given a choice: Stay in the bus all day or climb a 13,000-foot mountain. As soon as the options were given, I heard the contest begin. Some of Dawn's friends tried to convince her to stay in the bus with them.

Meanwhile, the others attempted to coax her to join them in their hike up the peak. In order to understand the full magnitude of the struggle

that was transpiring, one needs to know that Dawn was a rather large young lady. Her size would make an already difficult climb all the more challenging. Dawn's "to the top" friends assured her that they would support her throughout the climb and that they would make sure she would conquer the pinnacle. With this pledge ringing in her ears, Dawn left the bus with her more aspiring friends who quickly surrounded her and began calling out words of encouragement.

On at least two occasions, we stopped to rest. The calm of these moments was broken, however, as the sound of Dawn and her motivational entourage gradually caught up with the lead group. Finally, the main cluster reached the summit (because it was there!). I cannot put into words the splendor of what my eyes beheld as I soaked in the beauty of God's creation from the pinnacle.

As I was lost in the grandeur of it all, a cheer suddenly broke out from the ranks and the crowd began to part. There was Dawn, making her way to the top with her true friends continuing their encouraging cheers: "You can do it!" "Just a few more steps!" "We knew you'd make it!" It seemed as though time stood still as the rest of us watched Dawn reach the top and take a sweeping panorama of the view. Grinning from ear to ear, she proceeded to clutch her friends in her arms as they joined together in a deep and meaningful group embrace.

"A friend is one who comes in when the whole world has gone out."

—Anonymous Jr.

We all eventually made it down the mountain again (because it was there). On the bus were Dawn's other friends, bored to tears and oblivious to what had transpired at the top of the mountain. I learned a valuable lesson that day with Dawn on the side of a mountain: Choose your friends wisely, because you will end up where your friends are going. The difference between Dawn staying at the bottom or making it to the top depended entirely on whom she chose to hang around. The same is true with you. Whether you make it to the top in life or stay at the bottom will be incredibly affected by whom you choose as your climbing partners.

Solomon warns us about the power of a friend's influence when he declares, *"He who walks with the wise grows wise, but a companion of fools suffers harm"* (Proverbs 13:20). Perhaps this is where we get the phrase,

"It's hard to soar like an eagle when you hang around turkeys." Both sayings are true. I know of two young women who are very similar in several respects. Both were relatively new believers who had been dating their non-Christian boyfriends for years. Both girls were confronted with the realization that their boyfriends were not interested in giving their lives to the One who had transformed theirs. Moreover, both young women were becoming acutely aware that their boyfriends were bringing them down and that a decision was necessary: walk with Christ or follow the fella. Here is where the similarities end.

One gal made the difficult, painful decision to part company with the dude in order that she might grow in Christ—and grow she did. Imagine a chart with the arrow climbing drastically and you have an idea of how her faith and life appeared to take off. Sadly, this was not the case with Young Lady Number Two. Her decision was to date the dude and stand up the Savior. Imagine another chart with the arrow descending dramatically and you begin to get the picture of how her devotion to Christ appeared to decline. The good news is that Young Lady Number Two eventually saw what was happening and waved goodbye to the "friend" who was dragging her under. As a result, her faith has ignited, and her chart has completely changed directions.

I hope to see you at the top of life's mountain. Choose your climbing partners well.

"A friend will joyfully sing with you when you are on the mountaintop, and silently walk beside you through the valleys."

—Anonymous III

re ACTION

■ Spiritually, are you a thermometer or a thermostat? Do you become the temperature or set the temperature of the environment you are in?

■ What are the qualities of a good friend?

■ If you were another person, would you like to be a friend of yours? Why or why not?

■ Think about your Christian life as a journey up a mountain. Which of your current friendships are taking you higher?

■ Being as specific as possible, tell how these friends have been helpful climbing partners.

■ Be honest: Are there any friendships that are hindering your climb or dragging you away from Christ?

■ I Corinthians 15:33 says, *"Do not be misled: 'Bad company corrupts good character.'"* How would you explain this verse to a friend hanging around the wrong crowd?

"A friend loves at all times, and a brother is born for adversity."

—Proverbs 17:17

"A man of many companions may come to ruin, but there is a friend who sticks closer than a brother."   —Proverbs 18:24

"The dearest friend on earth is a mere shadow compared with Jesus Christ."   —Oswald Chambers

Reaching Out: Growing in Our Relationship with the World

day nine >>> **faith sharing**
day ten >>> **faith defending**
day eleven >>> **faith living**

section

4

day 9 > > >

The Domino Effect

"Give a man a dollar, and you cheer his heart. Give him a dream, and you challenge his heart. Give him Christ, and you change his heart."

—Anonymous

"The glory of God, and, as our only means to glorifying Him, the salvation of human souls, is the real business of life." —C.S. Lewis

"You will receive power when the Holy Spirit comes upon you and you will be my witnesses."

—Acts 1:8

The following is the complicated story of how I discovered pizza, or what I like to call "the domino effect." I'm not referring to the pizza place, but the game with the square game pieces with the little dots on them. One popular domino game is to stand individual dominoes back to back on their ends in an intricate pattern and then to tap the last domino in line. This sets off a cascading chain reaction as one by one they topple. Here's how I learned to love pizza:

It all started when Blanche introduced Peggy to Ray. To be more accurate, it really began when my uncle Roy met, fell in love with, and married Blanche, who then met Ray (Roy's younger brother). Blanche worked at a factory with Peggy. Now pay attention or you'll get lost. Blanche played matchmaker and convinced Ray to go on a blind date with Peggy.

As a result of that particular date, Ray and Peggy eventually fell in love, were married, and produced two adorable boys, Tim and Andy. You need to focus, because this is where it gets complicated. Gaye (Peggy's brother's wife) offered a slice of pizza to Peggy's brother's wife's nephew, Andy (also known as Ray's son, Roy's nephew, and Tim's brother), who for the very first time sampled this scrumptious concoction of dough, tomato sauce, cheese, and pepperoni. This began my lifelong addiction to pizza. Blanche introduced Ray to Peggy, which ultimately led me to *pizza*!

Have you ever considered the chain reaction that can happen when you introduce someone to Christ? I know of a wonderful, humble widow who invited her neighbor to church. Her neighbor was a shy little nine-year-old girl. Every Sunday, this little girl, who lived with an abusive parent, came to church with this caring widow and learned about a Heavenly Father who loved her enough to send His Son to die in her place.

In time, this little girl received Christ as her Lord and Savior. She immediately began to tell her mother about Jesus. Through this young girl's words, her mother came to Christ as well. Shortly thereafter, her brothers also bowed their knee to Christ. Nine years later, her father asked Jesus into his heart. This man had been an abusive, rage-filled alcoholic, yet from the moment of his conversion until his death, he never took another drink. Moreover, that little girl's father tirelessly shared Christ with those in his neighborhood and at work for the remainder of his life.

Not only did her father develop into a bold witness for the Gospel, her brothers became evangelists and pastors. Only God knows how many families have been restored, addictions conquered, hearts mended, prayers answered, hopes resurrected, and souls saved—all because a little old lady invited her nine-year-old neighbor to hear about Jesus.

Although most Christians understand the importance of sharing their faith, most feel woefully inadequate for the task. They genuinely question, "How can I be a witness for Jesus? After all, I've only been a Christian a short time." We have some good news for you: Some of the most effective faith-sharers in the Bible were brand-spanking new believers.

For instance, in the fifth chapter of Mark, we meet a demon-filled man who spent his days and nights running around a cemetery in his birthday suit. Jesus addressed him, delivered him, and then commissioned him, saying, *"Go home to your family and tell them how much the Lord has done for you and how he has had mercy on you"* (Mark 5:19). You and I have been given the same simple assignment: to go and tell others what Christ has done for us. Be encouraged by the fact that if God can use a recently delivered, abusive, possessed, wailing streaker to bring people to Himself, rest assured that He can use you and me as well.

Let's take a look at another example of God using ordinary people to bring people to His Son. In John 1:40 we see Andrew leading his brother Peter to Christ. You will note that he does nothing spectacular. You will find no flowery sermon or altar call. Andrew simply told his brother about his life-changing personal encounter with the Messiah and shared with Pete how he could have a similar experience.

This simple invitation would eventually lead to Peter coming to Christ, which would lead to two books of the Bible being authored and countless numbers of people coming to faith. Can you hear the dominoes falling? The point is that you don't have to be formally trained in evangelism or go to seminary to be an effective witness. A witness in a court of law simply explains what he or she has personally experienced. A witness for Christ does the same thing. That means that all that is necessary for you to be an effective witness for Christ is a willingness to share what He has done for you.

"When God is seeking a person, he will not allow my fear, my feeling of intimidation or my lack of knowledge or experience to prevent that person from finding him."
—Rebecca Manley Pippert

The truth is, each of us is constantly witnessing about various things. We testify to others all the time about a good movie, a great restaurant, our favorite team, or a certain sale. Grandmothers might be the greatest witnesses in the world. It is a foregone conclusion that anyone who spends time around a grandmother will undoubtedly be inundated with photos of the grandbaby.

What causes these otherwise normal ladies to be so eager to show both friends and complete strangers picture after picture of little Freddy spitting up? Does somebody force them to do this? Are there federal laws that mandate grannies to share with anything that has breath (and even the occasional inanimate object) the pictures and stories of their little darlings?

No, it's simply that they can't help but share about the precious child who has so captivated their heart. The fact of the matter is, we will be a witness. The only questions are, "For who or what are we witnessing?" and "Will we be faithful witnesses for the One who captivated our hearts and saved souls?"

"Witnessing is not a spare-time occupation or a once-a-week activity. It must be a quality of life. You don't go witnessing; you are a witness."
—Dan Greene

We should share our faith for four primary reasons:

1> God commands us to share the good news of salvation:

"Therefore go and make disciples of all nations, baptizing them in the name of the Father and of the Son and of the Holy Spirit, and teaching them to obey everything I have commanded you. And surely I am with you always, to the very end of the age." —(Matthew 28:19–20)

The Great Commission isn't a suggestion. Our God requires this of us. As Christians, we need no other reason than our Lord telling us to do so.

2> We can't help it.

Telling someone about Jesus should be a natural result of a growing relationship with Him. Nobody needs to command a high school boy to tell his companions about his new hot rod. He can't help it. He feels compelled to inform everybody about every detail: the luster of the paint, the horsepower of its engine, and the wattage of the stereo. You could threaten him with additional homework for life or inform him that you'd rather eat upholstery than hear about his car again, and he will still drone on and on about his new ride.

Likewise, if we are truly and passionately in love with Christ, we can't help but tell people about Him. We can't *not* tell people about Him. People could threaten us, mock us, or ignore us, but that wouldn't keep us from sharing about the One who set us free from sin and death.

"If you live by the same values and priorities [Jesus] had, you will find evangelism happening naturally. It becomes a lifestyle and not a project."
— Rebecca Manley Pippert

3> The task is so vital.

We've been given an awesome responsibility and opportunity. We possess the message of eternal life. How could we possibly keep such an incredibly important message to ourselves? If we possessed the cure for AIDS or cancer, it would be criminal for us to keep silent about such life-giving information. How much more heartless is it to withhold from people how they can have their sins forgiven, how they can find meaning and purpose in this mixed up world, how they can be freed from an eternity in hell, and how they can live forever in heaven when they pass from this life?

"The salvation of a single soul is more important than the production or preservation of all the epics and tragedies in the world."
— C.S. Lewis

4> The blessings are so great.

What could possibly be better than knowing that you played a part in changing where a person will spend eternity? What could possibly be cooler than having somebody come up to you in heaven and inform you that they are there because God used you to lead them to His Son? In Philemon 6, Paul says, *"I pray that you may be active in sharing your faith, so that you will have a full understanding of every good thing we have in Christ."* Ponder that for a moment. Paul is saying that in order for us to comprehend fully and experience all the blessings of God, we must be actively sharing our faith. We can say from experience that nothing, and we do mean nothing, turns our crank and blesses our hearts like seeing people come to Christ.

"Surely there can be no deeper joy than that of saving souls."

—Lottie Moon

FUEL

"You are to go into all the world and preach the good news to every-one, everywhere."

—Mark 16:15

"I planted the seed, Apollos watered it, but God made it grow."

—1 Corinthians 3:6

re**ACTION**

■ Who planted the Gospel in your heart, and how did it happen?

■ Was there anyone who "tilled" the soil before the Gospel was planted?

■ Think of a person with whom you could begin to share your faith in Christ.

Which of the following ways might be your next step?

❑ Invite him to youth, worship, or a church activity.

❑ Ask how she is doing and sincerely listen.

❑ Offer a prayer for a problem or situation in her life.

❑ Tell him how you came to Christ.

❑ Go shopping, play golf, rent a movie, or do anything together that could build a genuine friendship.

❏ Give him a great Christian book and/or say something to "fuel" his journey toward Christ.
❏ Pray for her. Pray for her soul. Pray for opportunities for her to hear the Gospel and for you to share the Gospel.

■ If your friend came to Christ, what are the possible domino effects? How might it change his or her home life or relationships?

■ How might sharing your faith have a chain reaction in your life?

 HIGHLY RECOMMENDED READING:

❏ *How to Give Away Your Faith* by Paul Little
❏ *Becoming a Contagious Christian* by Bill Hybels
❏ *Out of the Saltshaker and into the World* by Rebecca Manley Pippert
❏ *Faith Sharing* by H. Eddie Fox and George E. Morris

"What makes us Christians shrug our shoulders when we ought to be flexing our muscles? What makes us apathetic in a day when there are loads to lift, a world to be won and captives to be set free? Why are so many bored when the times demand action?"

—Billy Graham

d a y 1 0 › › ›

Apologetics: Can I Avoid It If I Wash My Hands?

"God is Dead."   —Fredrick Wilhelm Nietzsche

"Nietzsche is Dead."   —God

The battle over the truth of Christ has raged for two millennia. This clash of world-views has been a no-holds-barred, caged death match from the beginning.

"IN THIS CORNER...weighing in at 300 pounds...The Sultan of Sham... The Freakazoid of Fraud...The Heavyweight of Half-Truths...Slammin' Jammin' Secularism."

"AND IN THIS CORNER...at six-foot five inches of fightin' faith...The Titan of Truth...The Double Back Flip, Pile-Driven, Figure Four-Leg-Lockin' Defeater of Deception...Slayer of Pseudo-Science...a Chip off the Original Rock...pronounced defeated over one hundred times, only to rise up every time and kick some humanistic heinie...APOLLOOOOOOOOOOOOO THE APOOOOLOGIST!"

"Let's get it on..."

For 2,000 years, philosophers, politicians, and ordinary people have argued that the claims of Christianity are false. Everyone from Nietzsche to Madeline Murray O'Hare to your local college professor has predicted the demise or pronounced the irrelevance of the Biblical message. During these same 2,000 years, however, pastors, theologians, and plain, ordinary believers have defended the truth of the Gospel. Those persons who argue for the validity of our faith are called "apologists," and what they do is called apologetics.

One of the greatest defenders of the faith was an Oxford English professor named C.S. Lewis. He said, "To be ignorant and simple now—not to be able to meet the enemies on their own ground—would be to throw down our weapons. Good philosophy must exist, if for no other reason, because bad philosophy needs to be answered." In other words, a lie unanswered often times becomes accepted as truth. For this reason, the battle must be fought and the faith must be defended. How then can we stand up for the truth? The apostle Peter gave early Christians this advice:

> *"But in your hearts set apart Christ as Lord. Always be prepared to give an answer to everyone who asks you to give the reason for the hope you have. But do this with gentleness and respect, keeping a clear conscience..."* (1 Peter 3:15a).

What does that mean for us today? What does it mean when matters of faith get challenged at the lunch table, the water fountain, or in the classroom? Let's take a closer look at Peter's advice in this verse:

V E R S E : *"But in your hearts set apart Christ as Lord."*

P R I N C I P L E : **If we are to defend the faith, we must be faithful.**

R E A C T I O N : Our talk must match our walk. No matter how reasonable and convincing we are, if our lives aren't in sync with our words, no one will be persuaded. A genuine Christian life lived out, not necessarily in perfection, but in true sincerity, matters a whole lot more than being able to "win" an argument.

"Show me that you are redeemed, and I will believe in your Redeemer."

—Friedrich Wilhelm Nietzsche

V E R S E : *"Always be prepared to give an answer to everyone who asks you to give the reason for the hope you have."*

P R I N C I P L E : **If we are to defend the faith, we must be prepared.**

R E A C T I O N : First, we must become a lifelong student of the Bible. Now, that is not to say you must become a biblical scholar, fluent in Greek and Hebrew. However, we'll never be able to defend the faith effectively without studying the Bible. Here's a good goal to get you started: Know the Bible better today than you did yesterday. If you show up for a food fight with a spoon and three green peas, you're going to get creamed. Likewise, if you enter into a discussion about faith without having done your homework, you might leave with some emotional Jell-O in your hair. Having said this, remember that if you wait until you know all the answers before you defend the faith, you'll never defend the faith. Even when you do your homework, you'll occasionally have to scoop tapioca pudding out of your ears. So don't be afraid, trust in God, tell what you know, and keep trying to know more.

Second, you don't have to reinvent the wheel. Learn from some of the great minds who have defended the faith throughout history. Here are some books that can help:

- ❑ *More Than A Carpenter* and *Evidence that Demands a Verdict* by Josh McDowell
- ❑ *A Case for Christ* and *A Case for Faith* by Lee Stroble
- ❑ *Baker's Encyclopedia of Christian Apologetics* by Norman Geisler

"Be to the world a sign that while we as Christians do not have all the answers, we do know and care about the questions."

—Billy Graham

V E R S E : *"But do this with gentleness and respect, keeping a clear conscience, so that those who speak maliciously against your good behavior in Christ may be ashamed of their slander."*

P R I N C I P L E : **If we are to defend the faith, we must present our case in a gentle, loving, and respectful manner.**

R E A C T I O N : You can win the argument and lose the person. The most visible arguments for Christianity are Christians. The most visible arguments against Christianity are Christians. The old saying is true: People don't care what you know until they know that you care. The doubts and questions people raise often have more to do with bruised hearts than confused minds. **Also, if we are to defend the faith, we must repair the heart before we can address the mind.** Genuine Christian love is still the most persuasive argument of all.

"Men look for better methods, but God looks for better men."

—Erwin W. Lutzer

"Be wise in the way you act toward outsiders; make the most of every opportunity. Let your conversation be always full of grace, seasoned with salt, so that you may know how to answer everyone."

—Colossians 4:5–6

"Lord, let me lovingly and boldly stand up for Your truth..."

day 11 › › ›

The Best Disguise

"Your attitude must be like my own, for I [Jesus] did not come to be served, but to serve..." —Matthew 20:28 (*The Living Bible*)

We all long for heaven where God is but we have it in our power to be in heaven with Him right now—to be happy with Him at this very moment. But being happy with Him now means: loving as He loves, helping as He helps, giving as He gives, serving as He serves, rescuing as He rescues, being with Him for all the twenty-four hours, touching Him in His distressing disguise. —Mother Teresa

With many more children attending than we had anticipated, the costume party was a great success. The room was full of red and green balloons, screaming and laughing five year olds, yellow and blue streamers, six year olds sneezing into (and swapping) plastic masks, vivid and recently-mutilated decorations, seven year olds sweating profusely in partially-removed costumes, four hundred pounds of sugar-filled snacks, eight year olds wearing smeared face paint, six gallons of "radioactive green" punch, blaring music, one "adult" volunteer in a curly blue clown wig, three elderly women volunteers with permed blue hair, four Tinkerbells, three Elvises, six hobos, four farmers, three Sampsons, one Moses, and a partridge in a pear tree (well, at least a kid dressed up like a bird). The costume contest, however, was undoubtedly the highlight of the evening's festivities. After last year's "Snow White got a trophy, but I didn't" brawl, the organizers had the foresight to arrange enough prizes to ensure that each child received an award. Categories included funniest, most creative, wildest, cutest, silliest, and best homemade costume, just to name a few. As each child stood before the judges, some youngster would invariably say something like, "I bet you don't know who I am!" To which one of the judges would reply, "Well, who *could* that be behind that mask?"

One delightful little tyke, with a Sylvester the Cat mask on, marched up to the judge and announced boisterously, "Grandma, you'll never guess in a million years who I am." This grandmother/costume judge only had one grandson, whom she babysat five days a week. She absolutely adored the little fellow, talked about him continuously, and could have easily identified his voice even if he were clothed in full scuba gear, placed in armor, and wrapped in toilet paper in a stadium full of identically costumed children. With a performance worthy of an Academy award, she pulled up his mask and feigned surprise as she questioned, "Chad, is that you?" She then quickly proceeded to hug the dickens out of the little guy.

In the twenty-fifth chapter of Matthew, the Bible says,

"For I was hungry and you gave me something to eat."

For 2,000 years, Christians have been challenged to look beyond the mask.

"I was thirsty and you gave me something to drink."

When other students see an "odd" kid sitting by herself in the cafeteria, we are called to look behind the mask and see Christ.

"I was a stranger and you invited me in."

When this culture sees a hopeless drug addict, we are to look beneath the facade and see the image of Jesus.

"I needed clothes and you clothed me."

When you hand a plate of food to a homeless man at a soup kitchen, you touch Christ in His "distressing disguise."

"I was sick and you looked after me."

When the world sees a frail child in a distant land, we are to lift up the mask and recognize the One who is near and dear.

"I was in prison and you came to visit me."

We are called to minister to the hungry, the homeless, and the hurting, to serve without expecting credit or a reward, and to love the unlovable.

"Then the righteous will answer him, 'Lord, when did we see you hungry and feed you, or thirsty and give you something to drink? When did we see you a stranger and invite you in, or needing clothes and clothe you? When did we see you sick or in prison and go to visit you?' The King will reply, 'I tell you the truth, whatever you did for one of the least of these brothers of mine, you did for me.'"

Martin of Tours was a Christian Roman soldier. On a bitterly cold day, a beggar approached him requesting a handout. Martin searched deep in his pockets, but found no money to give the shivering man. Although his soldier's coat was warn and ragged, Martin reasoned that half an old coat was better than nothing to give to the man. Martin proceeded to slice his jacket in two and gave half to the grateful beggar. That same evening, Martin dreamed he went to heaven. He saw the streets of gold, a myriad of angels, and, most important, His Lord. He couldn't help but notice that Jesus was wearing half a coat of a Roman soldier. Martin overheard one angel question the Lord as to why He was wearing such a dilapidated jacket and how He had acquired it. The Lord answered with a smile, "My servant Martin gave it to me." Amazing, isn't it? Jesus asserts that when we love someone or touch someone or serve someone in His name, in actuality, we are loving, touching, and serving Him.

The big question is *how*? In a world with so many hurting people, how can I make a difference? What could little old me possibly do to help, and where would I even begin? On any given day, each of us might encounter dozens or even hundreds of people who could use our assistance. If we aren't careful, we could become so overwhelmed by our inability to do everything that we end up doing nothing.

We are not the first Christians to be bowled by the sheer enormity of the sickness, pain, suffering, violence, emptiness, and loneliness we see in the world around us. Listen to the advice of those who rolled up their sleeves and reached out their hands in Christian love. As you read these quotations, keep in mind that these men and women were ordinary folks whom God used in extraordinary ways, simply because they were willing to get Gospel under their fingernails.

"Do all the good you can, by all the means you can, in all the ways you can, in all the places you can, at all the times you can, to all the people you can, as long as ever you can."
—John Wesley

"I long to accomplish a great and noble task, but it is my chief duty and joy to accomplish humble tasks as though they were great and noble. For the world is moved along, not only by the mighty shoves of its heroes, but also by the aggregate of tiny pushes of each honest worker." —Helen Keller

"Do not think me mad. It is not to make money that I believe a Christian should live....The noblest thing a man can do is, just humbly to receive, and then go amongst others and give." —David Livingstone

"I am just a little pencil in God's hands...Doing something beautiful for God." —Mother Teresa

"If I could give you information of my life it would be to show how a woman of very ordinary ability has been led by God in strange and unaccustomed paths to do in His service what He has done in her. And if I could tell you all, you would see how God has done all, and I nothing. I have worked hard, very hard, that is all; and I have never refused God anything." —Florence Nightengale

"Do little things as if they were great because of the majesty of the Lord Jesus Christ who dwells in you; and do great things as if they were little and easy because of his omnipotence." —Blaise Pascal

"Many people neglect the task that lies at hand and are content with having wished to do the impossible." —Teresa of Avila

All these saints have a common attitude and approach to life. Mother Teresa saw Christ in the faces around her. Helen Keller trusted in the Holy Spirit to give her strength for the task. John Wesley did what he could, with what he had, where he was. Though Florence Nightingale saw enormous pain and hurt in her society, she did not become paralyzed by the magnitude of the problems around her, but was empowered by the enormity of the God within her. The next time you are tempted to be discouraged by the pachyderm-sized needs around you, just remember how you eat an elephant: one bite at a time.

FUEL

"Let us not become weary in doing good, for at the proper time we will reap a harvest if we do not give up. Therefore, as we have opportunity, let us do good to all people, especially to those who belong to the family of believers."

             —Galatians 6:9–10

"Which of these three do you think was a neighbor to the man who fell into the hands of robbers?" The expert in the law replied, 'The one who had mercy on him.' Jesus told him, 'Go and do likewise.'"

             —Luke 10:36–37

"The King will reply, 'I tell you the truth, whatever you did for one of the least of these brothers of mine, you did for me.' "Then he will say to those on his left, 'Depart from me, you who are cursed, into the eternal fire prepared for the devil and his angels. For I was hungry and you gave me nothing to eat, I was thirsty and you gave me nothing to drink, I was a stranger and you did not invite me in, I needed clothes and you did not clothe me, I was sick and in prison and you did not look after me.' They also will answer, 'Lord, when did we see you hungry or thirsty or a stranger or needing clothes or sick or in prison, and did not help you?' He will reply, 'I tell you the truth, whatever you did not do for one of the least of these, you did not do for me.' Then they will go away to eternal punishment, but the righteous to eternal life."

             —Matthew 25:40–46

reACTION

■ Where in your life can you look behind a mask to see the face of Jesus?

■ Who in your life has the greatest immediate need?

■ What practical actions can you do to help?

■ Here are some additional reACTIONS to try:

❑ Skip renting a flick and give the money saved to a prison ministry.

❑ Volunteer at a homeless shelter or a crisis assistance shelter.

❑ Give an old coat to the Salvation Army. Or give a new coat to the Salvation Army.

❑ Ask a school principal if you could donate school supplies to a needy student.

PRAYER starter

"Lord Jesus, help me to see Your face everywhere I look today…"

day 12 › › ›

Power Failure

"But you will receive power when the Holy Spirit comes on you...."

—Acts 1:8

t's a dark and stormy night. Your computer keys are smokin' as you bring to brilliant completion the term paper on weather patterns for your earth science class, which you have foolishly entitled, "The Loch Ness Monster and Other Sightings of Elvis." Suddenly, a blinding bolt of lightning zigzags across the sky and strikes Sparky's dog chain sending him sailing into the Johnson's pool. (Sparky's fine, and when you hold his tail just right, you can pick up three FM stations.) The electricity runs straight from Sparky's chain into your house, melting your surge suppressor and sending your hard drive, along with your nearly completed term paper, careening through your den window and into the Johnson's pool. Now your computer keys are literally smokin', and the powerfully combined smell of ozone, burning plastic, and singed dog hair permeates the room.

If this happened to you, would you continue typing? Of course not. How stupid would it be to continue pounding away on powerless computer keys in the dark? In the same way, people are pounding away, feebly attempting to live the Christian life without the power to do so. We know in our hearts that we *should* and we *ought*, but in reality, we can't and we won't. Through sheer determination we have tried to be more Christ-like, but we have painfully discovered that in our own strength, we can't even imitate Michael Jordan, much less Jesus Christ.

"The biggest blessing in your life was when you came to the end of trying to be a Christian, the end of reliance on natural devotion, and were willing to come as a pauper and receive the Holy Spirit."

—Oswald Chambers

Face it, most of us suffer from spiritual power failure. The good news is that, through the Holy Spirit, God makes available to us all the power we will ever need to live the life to which He calls us. During the next five studies, we will take a look at the person and work of God's Holy Spirit within our lives.

Who or what is the Holy Spirit? First, He is not "The Force." He is not some impersonal power. Second, "He" is not an "It." Jesus never referred to the Holy Spirit as "It" but as "He." Third, He is God. He is the third member of the Trinity along with the Father and the Son. Fourth, He is sent to us to equip and empower us to act and minister as Christians.

In the early 1900s, a guy won a car in a raffle. He'd never seen an automobile before, so after he received his prize, he tied his two horses to the front bumper and pulled his new car through the streets, never realizing there was an engine under the hood. We snicker at the thought of someone doing such a whacky thing. However, attempting to live the Christian life in our own meager strength, when the power of Almighty God is available to us, is even crazier. Is there a difference between a self-powered life and a Spirit-empowered life? Is there a difference between a horse and buggy and the space shuttle?

Imagine two gloves. One is lying on a table while the other is filled with a person's hand. The first glove simply exists. It is still a glove, but it is not empowered to do what a glove was created to do. The other glove, however, is filled and empowered by that hand, and its capabilities are limitless. Those two gloves tell a story about our lives. God has designed and created us to be filled and empowered by the Spirit of God. We will be true to our purpose only when we are empowered by the Spirit.

In Acts 1:8, we learn that *"we will receive power"* when the Holy Spirit comes upon us. The word used for "power" in that verse is "dunamis," which is the root word for our English word "dynamite." God is saying that there is dynamic power available in the Holy Spirit.

Why do we need power as Christians? I'm glad you asked. We need power to obey. We need power to say "yes" to the things we should say "yes" to and "no" to the things we should say "no" to. We need power to handle pressure. We also need power to minister and to witness. In Acts 1:4, Jesus told His disciples not to try to do anything without first being empowered by His Spirit. In other words, Jesus is saying, *don't attempt to live the Christian life without the power necessary to accomplish that life.*

"God commands us to be filled with the Spirit, and if we are not filled, it is because we are living beneath our privileges." —D.L. Moody

---

FUEL

"[D]o not leave Jerusalem, but wait for the gift my Father promised, which you have heard me speak about. For John baptized with water, but in a few days you will be baptized with the Holy Spirit."

—Acts 1:4–5

P E T E R , B E F O R E the power of the Holy Spirit in His life:

"Now Peter was sitting out in the courtyard, and a servant girl came to him. 'You also were with Jesus of Galilee,' she said. But he denied it before them all. 'I don't know what you're talking about,' he said."

—Matthew 26:69–70

P E T E R , A F T E R the power of the Holy Spirit in His life:

"With many other words he warned them; and he pleaded with them, 'Save yourselves from this corrupt generation.' Those who accepted his message were baptized, and about three thousand were added to their number that day."

—Acts 2:40–41

"Then Peter said, 'Silver or gold I do not have, but what I have I give you. In the name of Jesus Christ of Nazareth, walk.' Taking him by the right hand, he helped him up, and instantly the man's feet and ankles became strong."

—Acts 3:6–7

"Peter sent them all out of the room; then he got down on his knees and prayed. Turning toward the dead woman, he said, 'Tabitha, get up.' She opened her eyes, and seeing Peter she sat up. He took her by the hand and helped her to her feet. Then he called the believers and the widows and presented her to them alive." —Acts 9:40–41

re**ACTION**

■ In what area do you most need the Holy Spirit to empower you today?

❑ Speech/conversation.   ❑ Strength to forgive.
❑ Boldness to witness.   ❑ Serving in ministry.
❑ Avoiding temptation.   ❑ Loving the unlovable.
❑ Other (specify): _____

■ What best describes your experience with the Holy Spirit so far? Why?

❑ Static cling.
❑ Firecracker.
❑ Dynamite.

■ Describe an experience when you've been most aware of the presence of the Holy Spirit.

PRAYER starter

"Holy Spirit, I don't have the power to live the
Christian life apart from You, so I ask You to..."

day 13 > > >

The Bachelor Pad

"Holiness is inwrought by the Holy Spirit, not because we have suffered, but because we have surrendered." —Richard Shelley Taylor

As you walk up the driveway to your now-former bachelor pad with your new bride, a thought seeps through your testosterone-clouded mind: *I probably should have cleaned up.* In actuality, you did attempt to straighten up once, but that was during the Reagan administration. As you open the door and carry her across your threshold, you warn, "It might be a *little* messy." Those words constitute the first lie you have told your new wife.

As she surveys her new home for the first time, her inhaling gasp of shock is violent enough to affect tides in Venezuela. The floor is ankle-deep in pizza boxes left from the Paleolithic era and underwear from the Crustacean Period. Under the couch, there is enough dirt to support agriculture, which explains the lush fern nobody remembers bringing in. Her tear-filled eyes move from the floor to the wall. The wallpaper looks as though angry, drunken baboons flung it there. The velvet Elvis painting is tipped at such an angle that it almost appears he is singing to the dogs playing poker.

She begins to tip-toe cautiously around the room as though in a minefield. She spies the letter written by the workers at the sewage treatment plant next door complaining about the odor wafting over from your house. Suddenly she leaps back as a pizza box scurries toward her. "Sparky! So there you are! I thought you were dead!" you shout in delight. After a brief moment of hyperventilation, your new wife reaches her trembling hands toward the door of the refrigerator (or as you call it, "The Laboratory") only to witness biological warfare being waged between the Moo Gou Gai Pan and the "Salsa Sauerkraut Surprise." You take a moment to ponder pridefully how three different diseases have been simultaneously created and cured through the growth process of your "cheese." As she begins to gag, she foolishly runs toward the bathroom as you chase her, screaming, "In the name of all that is sacred, *don't go in there!*"

Thankfully, your new bride doesn't give up and head back to Mom and Dad. Instead, your new bride takes up residence with you, and the "Bachelor Pad from Hades" is transformed into a home suitable for human habitation through the loving hands of its new tenant. Likewise, when the Holy Spirit takes up residence in our lives, He wants to do some house cleaning.

During the two previous studies, we have examined how the Holy Spirit empowers and influences us. Now let's take a look at another work of the Holy Spirit in our lives.

The Holy Spirit S A N C T I F I E S U S

Both 1 Peter 1:2 and II Thessalonians 2:13 talk about the sanctifying work of the Spirit. What in the world does *sanctify* mean? It means "to set apart as special" and "clean up." Remember, He is the Holy Spirit and His desire is to make us holy as well. When the Holy Spirit fills our hearts, He sets out to clean us up. His desire is to get rid of the junk and filth that clutters and dirties our lives. In some rooms, the Holy Spirit lovingly and gently sweeps away the dust and cobwebs. But let's be honest—some of the rooms of our hearts are in such disarray that the dust bunnies have become dust bison and it requires an industrial strength leaf blower, so to speak, to push out this collection of garbage. Thankfully, we have an "industrial strength" God who can transform even the crustiest abodes into a habitat fit for the King of Kings.

"Holy has the same root as wholly, it means complete. A man is not complete in spiritual stature if all his mind, heart, soul, and strength are not given to God."
—R. J. Stewart

Let's be even more straightforward. There are rooms in our hearts that we have foolishly tried to hide from the Spirit or have attempted to keep off limits from His sanctifying work. A growing Christian will discover, however, that we stiff-arm this work of the Holy Spirit at our own peril. We will also discover that His persistent love compels Him to clean not only every room, but also under every bed, in every closet, and in every drawer.

Moreover, house cleaning is never truly finished in that there is always new dust and dirt to deal with; so it is with the dust and dirt of our hearts. This side of heaven, the Holy Spirit never ceases to dust, clean, and vacuum our lives in order to make us more like Jesus.

"Although we become Christians instantaneously by faith in Christ, knowing God and developing faith is a gradual process. There are no shortcuts to maturity. It takes time to be holy." —Erwin W. Lutzer

God loves us so much that He accepts us just as we are. But He also loves us too much to allow us to stay that way. He cleans us up.

FUEL

"Therefore do not let sin reign in your mortal body so that you obey its evil desires. Do not offer the parts of your body to sin, as instruments of wickedness, but rather offer yourselves to God, as those who have been brought from death to life; and offer the parts of your body to him as instruments of righteousness." —Romans 6:12–13

reACTION

■ As you give the Holy Spirit the key to His new home—your heart—what is the "room" in your life that needs the most attention? Would He:

❏ Shake out bitterness and unforgiveness?
❏ Sweep away selfishness and self-centeredness?
❏ Disinfect your lust and immorality?
❏ Wash away your fears and tears?
❏ Throw away ingratitude?
❏ Buff away a hardened heart?

■ How and where would the Holy Spirit redecorate your heart?

■ What's in your "closet" that you've tried to keep Him from straightening?

"Holiness means something more than the sweeping away of the old leaves of sin; it means the life of Jesus developed in us."

—I. Lilias Trotter

day 14 > > >

Under the Influence

*"Do not get drunk on wine, which leads to debauchery. Instead, be
filled with the Spirit."*
—Ephesians 5:18

D id you catch that? The Ephesians passage tells us that not only is it
God's desire for us to be filled with His Holy Spirit, but it is also His
command. Notice, too, that we are to "be filled." In other words,
being filled with the Spirit isn't something we do ourselves. Like salvation,
it is something that only God can do for us. But also like salvation, being
filled with God's Spirit requires our cooperation. Luke 11:13 tells us that
God gives the Holy Spirit *"to those who ask."*
In the original language, "filled" can mean a couple of things:

1> "Filled" can mean "permeated."

It is a brisk moonlit night as you and Snookiepookums are walking hand
in hand around the lake. You notice that she is shivering a bit in her T-shirt
as the snow begins to pile up around you. Being the chivalrous studmuf-
fin you are, you take off your down parka and your fleece-lined jacket and
offer her your sweatshirt (the one that sports, "My parents went to the
Andromeda Galaxy and all I got was this lousy sweatshirt."). She gladly accepts and you continue your walk. As you part ways for the evening, you
give her a healthy, firm handshake and she gives you back your sweatshirt

as you bid each other adieu for the evening.

The following day you throw on that same sweatshirt as you head to class. There is something different about it today, however. Amazingly, it doesn't smell like its normal combination of gym socks, Sparky's breath, and road kill. Instead, it smells like honeysuckle and jasmine, potpourri and lavender, a cool rain and cinnamon. Instead, it smells like...her. Her perfume has permeated your old, crusty sweatshirt, transforming it from foul to fragrant.

Similarly, God's Holy Spirit wants to permeate our lives and transform our old and crusty goals, motives, attitudes, and actions. Just as stirring sugar into iced tea affects every molecule of the tea, when God's Holy Spirit permeates our lives, He will begin to affect every area for good.

2> "Filled" can also be translated "controlled totally by."

When I answered the door, I was standing face to face with a very large, very irritated officer of the law. The youth group party I was hosting began innocently enough, but apparently, it soon got out of hand. After such raucous and "deviant" games as limbo, charades, and Pictionary, I guess we got a little loud. Someone had narked on us and alerted the authorities that wild, marauding, delinquent hooligans and Hottentots were having a "kegger" at my house. In reality, the strongest drink we were serving was a caffeinated soda. It didn't take long for the officer to discern that we were not inebriated. We were simply a harmless youth group with a serious case of the silly giggles.

The early church had the same problem. The joy and miracles that filled the church after the Holy Sprit came at Pentecost led the crowd to accuse them of being drunk (Acts 2:13). If you have ever seen someone inebriated, you have witnessed someone who was under the control of alcohol. The booze influences their speech, their thinking, and their actions. Ideally, when God's Spirit dwells in us, He will likewise have an affect on how we talk, how we think, and what we do.

Let's take a sobriety test. What are some of the signs of being under the influence of alcohol? You can't lean your head back and touch your nose. You can't walk a straight line. Your speech is slurred. Your reaction time is slowed to a crawl. You see double and your head spins.

On the other hand, in Galatians 5:22, Paul tells us that someone under the influence of the Holy Spirit will exhibit *"love, joy, peace, patience, kindness, goodness, faithfulness, gentleness, and self-control."*

"The Spirit's control will replace sin's control. His power is greater than the power of all your sin."

—Erwin W. Lutzer

The fact is we are going to be filled with something. Some people are filled with jealousy, others lust. Still others are filled with bitterness, anger, hatred, or greed. If we are going to be filled with something, is there anything better to be filled with than the very One with whom we were created to be filled? When He permeates our lives and we come under His loving, powerful control, our lives will never be the same again.

"If we are full of pride and conceit and ambition and self-seeking and pleasure and the world, there is no room for the Spirit of God, and I believe many a man is praying to God to fill him when he is full already with something else."

—D.L. Moody

FUEL

"These men are not drunk, as you suppose. It's only nine in the morning! No, this is what was spoken by the prophet Joel: 'In the last days, God says, I will pour out my Spirit on all people. Your sons and daughters will prophesy, your young men will see visions, your old men will dream dreams.'"

—Acts 2:15–17

reACTION

■ If you were given a "life-alizer" test, would there be enough evidence to convict you of living under the influence of the Holy Spirit?

■ We listed earlier the "fruit of the Spirit" from Galatians 5:22 (love, joy, peace, patience, kindness, faithfulness, gentleness, and self-control). Be your own fruit inspector: Which of these "fruit of the Spirit" are most evident in your life? Which are not so evident?

■ Describe a time within this past week when you have been under the Spirit's influence?

PRAYER starter

"Holy Spirit, please permeate every area of my life
and bring my life under Your total control..."

day 15 › › ›

A Ton of Bricks

"God is closest to those whose hearts are broken." —Jewish proverb

"God...is not in the business of helping the humanly strong become stronger; rather he takes the weak and makes them strong in himself."

—Erwin W. Lutzer

"And I [Jesus] will pray to the Father, and He shall give you another Comforter, that He may abide with you forever."

—John 14:16 (*King James Version*)

Although I had known for months that the phone call was eminent, it nevertheless hit me like a ton of bricks. My dad was on the other end of the phone informing me that my mother, who had bravely battled cancer for fourteen years, was at death's door. I was in college almost 800 miles away from home. My dad had booked me on the next flight out, in hopes that I would be able to say goodbye to my mother before she passed away.

I remember hanging up the phone ever so slowly and turning to look at myself in the mirror. A large part of my world was caving in and the pain in my heart was overwhelming. I looked at my reflection and cried out to God saying, "I can't handle this on my own." Suddenly, a peace enveloped me, and for the first time as a relatively new believer, I came to under-stand first-hand the comfort of God's Holy Spirit. Is that to say that I no longer hurt? Of course not. Did I still cry? Absolutely. Was it still difficult? Without question. But did I feel God's presence and comfort through it all? No doubt. It was on that terribly difficult day that I discovered that the Holy Spirit's comfort is wonderfully and perfectly sufficient.

"God does not leave us comfortless, but we have to be in dire need of comfort to know the truth of his promise. It is in time of calamity...in days and nights of sorrow and trouble that the presence, the suffi-ciency, and the sympathy of God grow very sure and very wonderful. Then we find out that the grace of God is sufficient for all our needs, for every problem, and for every difficulty, for every broken heart, and for every human sorrow."
—Peter Marshall

Not only does the Holy Spirit comfort us, He helps us. In John 14:16, Jesus told His disciples and us, *"I will ask the Father, and He will give you another Counselor to be with you forever."* The word used here for "Coun-selor" literally means "one called alongside to help."

"The weaker we feel, the harder we lean on God. And the harder we lean, the stronger we grow."
—Joni Eareckson Tada

Jesus is telling us that we never have to walk alone. In the 1992 Bar-celona Olympics, Derrick Redmond, a twenty-six-year-old British runner, was heavily favored in the 400-meter dash. As he raced through the back-stretch in his semi-final heat, Derrick felt a searing pain rip through his leg. Falling to the track, Derrick realized he had torn his hamstring. In one of the most memorable moments in Olympic history, Derrick clawed his way to a standing position and began to limp and hop painfully toward the finish line. While the crowd was mesmerized by this determined young man's valiant effort, a second person suddenly appeared in the drama.

This man, sporting a T-shirt bearing the words "Have you hugged your child today?" attempted to make his way through the security guards who were struggling to block his efforts to reach the hobbling athlete. After informing the guards who he was, Jim Redmond, Derrick's father, was permitted to run to his son. Once beside him, Jim wrapped his arm around the young man. At this point, the weight of the moment was too much for Derrick, and he began to sob on his dad's shoulder. "You don't have to do this," Jim said to his son. "Yes, I do," the young man replied. "Then we'll finish the race together." Many in the large crowd, now moved to tears, stood and cheered the compassion of the father and the courage of the son.

Let's face it, as humans there are times we sprint through life, there are times we jog through life, and there are times we limp through life. Never forget though, that there is One who runs alongside us, who encourages us, and when necessary, even carries us.

"The Lord doesn't promise to give us something to take so we can handle our weary moments. He promises us himself. That is all. And that is enough."

—Charles R. Swindoll

"Praise be to the God and Father of our Lord Jesus Christ, the Father of compassion and the God of all comfort, who comforts us in all our troubles, so that we can comfort those in any trouble with the comfort we ourselves have received from God. For just as the sufferings of Christ flow over into our lives, so also through Christ our comfort overflows."

—2 Corinthians 1:3–5

"But he said to me, 'My grace is sufficient for you, for my power is made perfect in weakness.' Therefore I will boast all the more gladly about my weaknesses, so that Christ's power may rest on me."

—2 Corinthians 12:9

"God does not comfort us to make us comfortable, but to make us comforters."

—John Henry Jowett

re**ACTION**

■ What is hitting you "like a ton of bricks" in your life right now?

■ Where do you most need God's help?

■ Who could you comfort today?

"No experience—neither that of joy nor of sorrow—is full and complete, until it is shared with God."—Michael Card

PRAYER starter

"Holy Spirit, I'm hurting..."

d a y 1 6 > > >

Warning Signals

> *"When [the Holy Spirit] comes, He will convict the world of guilt in regard to sin."*
>
> —John 16:8

> *"Conscience is a walkie-talkie set by which God speaks to us."*
>
> —James J. Metcalf

You're cruising your family down the highway in your new high-tech "Stealth Panzer" SUV, referred to by *Car and Yacht* magazine as "an oil tanker on wheels" (approximate miles per gallon: fourteen feet; estimated stopping distance at sixty miles per hour: Nebraska). You went all out and purchased the "Special Edition" with the cutting edge "NORAD Driving Enhancement" package, complete with every conceivable gadget known to man with the possible exception of phasers.

A few hours into your excursion, a warning light subtly fades in and out on the instrument panel. You choose to ignore it. A few minutes later, a barely audible, "ding, ding" begins to coincide with the flashing warning light. Again, you choose to disregard it. Exactly one minute later a lady's soothing voice announces, "Your vehicle's engine temperature is exceeding recommended safety limits. Please pull to the side of the road immediately." In an attempt to drown out the sound, you begin to hum in Latin. One minute later, the same voice, no longer so soothing, states "I SAID, the engine is getting hot—stop the car!" and the "ding, ding" is replaced with a more irritating, "BEEP! BEEP!"

At this point, you turn up the volume on the car stereo to the level in between "ear bleed" and "thermonuclear explosion." After fifteen more seconds, the voice, now sounding oddly like your mother's, addresses you by your full name and broadcasts, "Young man, if you don't pull this car over right this instant, you'll be grounded until the next presidential administration!" Before you have the chance to get into an argument with your dashboard, the windshield wiper fluid begins to spell out a message. At the same time, a fax scrolls down from the sun visor as an airbag banner inflates.

All three contain the following warning: "THE VEHICLE'S ENGINE HAS REACHED CRITICAL MASS. THE COMPUTER CORE HAS BEEN EJECTED, AND YOUR LEFT SHOE IS ON FIRE."

You now have three choices. You can:

1) Continue to ignore the warning signals once again and suffer the consequences.
2) Take out the sledgehammer concealed in the glove compartment (What do you mean you don't have a sledge concealed in there?!) and smash the begeebers out of the entire console while screaming, "This warning signal never lets me have any fun!"
3) Calmly think, *Hey, I must have a problem with my engine. I sure am glad that this sophisticated warning system activated and I didn't destroy my car.*

Likewise, the Holy Spirit will set off a warning signal within our hearts when something is amiss or potentially harmful. The Spirit forces us to choose between ignoring His warning and facing the consequences or heeding His admonition and being spared the suffering our sin will bring. Remember, God's motivation behind His conviction is always love. Loving parents will warn their child not to stick his or her finger in a light socket, kiss a glowing burner on the stove, play hopscotch on the interstate, or pet the big, long worm with the rattles on its tail. A parent does this, not to keep their children from fun, but to spare them from pain.

"Conscience warns us as a friend before it punishes us as a judge."

—King Leszczynski Stanislaw I

I play guitar. I still remember the first time I strained to push my fingers against the bronze and steel strings of my six-string in a feeble attempt to make music. It hurt. I'm not only referring to the auditory torture inflicted upon my poor neighbors, but also to the fact that my fingertips felt as though I had trimmed my nails with a ferret. The sensitive ends of my fingers were not used to such pressure, and they notified me as to their displeasure in no uncertain terms.

The next time I performed an unsolicited concert for my neighbors, however, it was somewhat less unbearable to press the strings due to my fingertips losing some of their sensitivity. A few weeks later, calluses had developed to such a degree that I could hardly feel the strings beneath my fingers any longer. Jesus reminds us that what had happened to my fingers can happen to people's hearts:

> *"For this people's heart has become calloused; they hardly hear with their ears, and they have closed their eyes"* (Matthew 13:15).

If we choose to ignore the Spirit's warning and lie to our parents, cheat on the exam, flirt with a co-worker who's not our spouse, miss church, or get drunk, conviction gnaws at us like a preacher eating fried chicken. But in a short time, the pain and the power of the guilt gradually fades. The second lie is easier than the first, and the uncomfortable flirtation becomes an inappropriate but unembarrassed embrace. If you give the devil a ride this week, next week he might be driving the SUV.

FUEL

"Because our gospel came to you not simply with words, but also with power, with the Holy Spirit and with deep conviction."

—1 Thessalonians 1:5

re**ACTION**

■ If the convicting power of the Holy Spirit could be compared to a car's warning system, what message would be flashing on your dash? Check the one that you need to pay attention to the most.

❑ "You're running low on spiritual fuel."

❑ "You're heading in the wrong direction."

❑ "Consult the owner's manual."

❑ "Put on the brakes!"

❑ "The consequences in your mirror may be closer than they appear."

■ Through what means might the Holy Spirit be trying to get your attention? Check one.

❑ Your parents.

❑ Your children.

❑ Your pastor.

❑ A Christian brother or sister.

❑ His "still small voice" (1 Kings 19:12).

❑ His Word.

❑ An incredible Christian book you are currently reading written by two strikingly good-looking authors.

PRAYER starter

"Lord, keep my spirit tender toward Your Spirit..."

Being Stewards of What God Has Given Us

section

6

d a y 17 > > >

It's About Time

> *"We master our minutes, or we become slaves to them; we use time, or time uses us."*
>
> —William A Ward

> *"Dost thou love life? Then do not squander time, for that's the stuff life is made of."*
>
> —Benjamin Franklin

I like the joke about the snail that was mugged by a gang of marauding turtles. The police questioned the snail as to what had happened and he responded, "Gee, I don't know...it all happened so fast." I also like the story about the group of guys who were whooping it up, slapping high-fives and giving each other congratulatory pats on the back. A lady asked them the reason for their raucous behavior, and one of the men replied, "We just finished a jigsaw puzzle, and it only took us six months." The lady retorted, "Six months? That sure seems like an awful long time to complete a puzzle." The guy countered by saying, "Long? It says on the front of the box 'four to six years'!"

Sometimes time can seem so relative, can't it? A week spent on vacation in Aruba seems quantitatively shorter than a week studying for finals. The last ten minutes of a really good movie go significantly faster than the last ten minutes before quitting time at work.

It has been stated that the most precious commodity today isn't gold, diamonds, or even weapons-grade plutonium—it's time. One of the most frequent statements that crosses our lips in this generation is, "I don't have time." Tragically, this declaration is usually in reference to those things that should be most important to us, such as God, family, and ministry. The old saying states that, "Time flies." Well, if it flies, where does it go?

According to statistics, if you live to be seventy-two years of age, you will spend:

- twenty-one years sleeping
- fourteen years working
- seven years participating in bathroom activities
- six years eating
- six years traveling
- five years waiting in line
- four years learning
- three years in meetings
- two years returning phone calls
- one year searching for lost things
- twenty-two months in worship
- eight months opening junk mail
- six months waiting at stop signs
- three months scolding children and
- eight days telling dogs to lie down and be quiet

Perhaps that is why the average married couple only spends four minutes a day talking, why the average dad only spends thirty seconds a day conversing with his children, why only thirty-seven percent of Americans read their Bibles, and why eighty percent of Christians have no ministry. Obviously, one of the greatest commodities God has made us stewards of is our time.

"What we love to do we find time to do." —John Lancaster Spalding

The good news is this: God will give us exactly as much time as we need to accomplish everything He calls us to do. Although Jesus only walked this earth for thirty-three years, and although He only had three years of public ministry, He was still able to say that He had completed all the work the Father gave Him (John 17:4). The problem is, although God gives us exactly as much time as we need to carry out all that He wills in our lives, we squander a bunch of that time holding back, attempting to negotiate, fighting God, and being plain old disobedient. I think we could all testify about time we have wasted hemming and hawing instead of being faithful to that which God has called us. I believe that one of the reasons that Jesus was able to make such a bodacious statement was that He allowed the Father to call the shots and prioritize His life. This is evidenced in His prayer in the Garden of Gethsemane. There He prayed, *"Not my will, but yours be done"* (Luke 22:42).

Likewise, if we want to be able to say we have fulfilled all that the Lord desired for us to accomplish when we come to the end of our lives, we too need to have that same submissive attitude toward the Lord. We don't have time to be everything God wants us to be and be constantly haggling with His plan.

"Don't be fooled with the calendar...there are only as many days of the year as we make use of. One person gets a week's value out of a year, while another gets a year's value out of a week."

—Charles Richards

The question then becomes: "How are we using the time we have been given?" Ephesians 5:16–17 tells us to, *"live with a due sense of responsibility, not as those who do not know the meaning of life, but as those who do. Make the best use of your time."* In order for this to happen, we must make today count. In other words, we need to "Carpe Diem" (Latin for "seize the carp" or "seize the day"). We need to wake up each day and give life our best, asking God to order our steps.

"A day is a miniature eternity."   —Ralph Waldo Emerson

"More important than length of life is how we spend each day."

—Maria A. Furtado

When you think about it, the only time we really have is the present. The opportunities we had in the past are gone. The opportunities we will have in the future are nothing more than a promissory note. But we do have today, and we have the opportunity to make today count. Jim Croche wrote and recorded the song "Time in a Bottle" way back in the 1970s. In this song he muses about the possibilities of saving up time for friends, family, and projects and storing it away for a later day.

The idea is that someday he would open up the bottle and grab a little time for the important things of life. While this idea might make for a pretty song, it makes for a lousy philosophy for living. One fateful day Jim tragically perished in a plane crash. Even if he could have found some mysterious way for bottling time, what would have happened to all the things he was planning on doing, all the people he was planning to know, and all the places he was planning on going? They would have gone up in flames and smoke when he did.

That is why it is so very important to share your faith today. Hug your kids or spouse or parents today. Reconcile a damaged relationship today. Read God's Word today. Love that person today. Quit playing games today. Because if we don't, there will come a day when we'll look back and give anything to do what we should have done days or weeks or years before.

A preacher once saw a sign outside a tree nursery that read, "The best time to plant a tree was 25 years ago. The second best time to plant a tree is today."

We can't reclaim lost opportunities, but we can use what we have been given today and act as wise stewards as we invest our time for God.

"It is precisely because of the eternity outside time that everything in time becomes valuable and important and meaningful. Therefore, Christianity...makes it of urgent importance that everything we do here (whether individually or as a society) should be rightly related to what we eternally are."
—Dorothy L. Sayers

FUEL

"Teach us to number our days, that we may gain a heart of wisdom."

—Psalm 90:12

"[T]oday, if you hear his voice, do not harden your hearts...."

—Hebrews 3:15

"There is a time for everything, and a season for every activity under heaven."

—Ecclesiastes 3:1

re**ACTION**

■ Where have you been attempting to save time in a bottle?

❏ Time with God.
❏ Time with family.
❏ Time in ministry.
❏ Time for a special project.
❏ Time for physical fitness.

■ What are your three biggest time wasters?

1)

2)

3)

■ What is one step this week you can take to start making better use of your time?

day 18 > > >

The Perfect Gift

> *"God has given each of us the ability to do certain things well."*
> —Romans 12:6 (*The Living Bible*)

> *"Eagerly desire spiritual gifts."*
> —1 Corinthians 14:1

You spent great quantities of time, energy, and money finding the perfect Christmas gift for your closest and dearest friend. This is the friend who took you to the emergency room when you sustained that deep gash on your forehead from the rabid gopher. Okay, this is also the friend who "double dog" dared you to stick your head in the gopher hole to begin with, but that's beside the point. Because of your close relationship, you are keenly aware of the joy that this "perfect" gift will bring to him, as well as the difference it will make in his life.

Christmas finally arrives. Early in the morning, you take off running to your friend's house to bestow this thought-filled present as quickly as possible. In your crazed zeal to deliver the goods, you leap over your neighbor's outdoor Christmas decorations, knocking down two shepherds and decapitating Blitzen. You are unfazed. You are on a mission. You can't wait to see his face as he opens the gift.

With one final superhuman effort, you hurdle Fang, your friend's toy poodle, and spring up his steps in a single bound. In your anxiousness, you ring the doorbell approximately twenty times per nano-second. At last, your friend appears at the door, and you thrust the gift into his hand with the speed of a person's head emerging from an enraged gopher's hole as you exclaim, "This is my special gift for you!"

You stand gazing in anticipation with a dorky smile pasted on your face as you wait for your amigo to rip into the present. But to your utter disappointment, your friend puts the gift on his dresser and says, "I think I'll open it later." The following summer, you spy the package peeking out from under your chum's bed, still unopened. How would you feel? Maybe that's how God feels when He grants us spiritual gifts that, for many Christians, sadly remain unopened and unused.

So what is a spiritual gift? A spiritual gift is a special God-given ability entrusted to believers to involve them in His Kingdom's mission.

There's an old saying, "Ignorance is bliss." Whoever said that was totally ignorant concerning what God says about spiritual gifts. **I Corinthians 12:1 says, *"Now about spiritual gifts, brothers, I do not want you to be ignorant."* Putting that in the positive:**

God wants you to know the spiritual gifts you have.

In high school, a friend coaxed me into playing a video game at a local arcade. I put my quarter in and set out to whoop up on some aliens from a distant galaxy. I furiously shot at them, hoping to see the simulated explosions of my simulated enemy's spaceships. Instead, my feeble bullets ricocheted harmlessly off of their seemingly invincible spacecrafts. All I had accomplished for my effort was to incur my simulated enemy's wrath as they tore into me like a youth group with a hot pepperoni pizza.

This process was swiftly repeated two times before the "Game Over" display flashed across the screen. I stared at the display in shock that I had been defeated so quickly and convincingly. My friend shook his head and questioned, "Why didn't you use your shields and your photon torpedoes?" In my less-than-nicest tone I responded, "Why didn't you tell me I had galactic shields and photon torpedoes?!" My comrade proceeded to show me the weapons at my disposal, and I stuck another quarter in the machine. This time E.T. was sweating as my blazing torpedoes made him wish he had never invaded our solar system.

What was the difference between my being waxed and my doing some waxing of my own? First, I became aware of the weapons at my disposal. Second, I used them. This is also the difference between a Christian who simply warms a pew on Sunday and a Christian who is whooping up on the kingdom of darkness.

God also wants you to be aware of the gifts you <u>don't</u> have.

Suppose you airlifted a cow that had been happily grazing in a lush field and you dropped her into the middle of the backstroke event at a swimming competition. How happy would Bessie be as a swimmer? Let me ask you another question: How effective would she be in the competition? She would be neither happy nor effective in an aquatic setting due to the fact that cows are udderly (ha!) horrible swimmers. They simply were never designed to do laps.

Now suppose you airlifted Shamu the whale and dropped her into the middle of the Gobi Desert. How happy would she be flopping around in the sand? She would probably feel like a fish (mammal) out of water. (ha, again!) How competent would she be trying to get around on land? She would be totally unhappy and totally ineffective as a land mammal due to the fact that she wasn't designed or created for such activity. On the other hand, if you put Bessie and Shamu back into the environments for which they were created, they will flourish. So do Christians.

Look around the average church and you'll see a lot of round pegs in square holes. You have people of all ages who are serving in areas where they are neither gifted nor passionate. As a result, these precious souls are frustrated because they don't like what they are doing and they see little positive fruits for their effort. Moreover, church leaders and the people they are serving are equally frustrated because things aren't working out according to plan, for obvious reasons. The tragedy in this is that those same people would be marvelous in other areas of service.

This is why God desires for each of us to be plugged into the ministries for which we have been equipped. Our spiritual gifts, passion, abilities, personalities, and experiences are tailor-made for certain ministries. When we find ourselves plugged into the niche for which we have been designed, we will have great satisfaction in and fruit from our ministry.

reACTION

Remember, God doesn't want us to be ignorant of spiritual gifts, so let's take a look on the following page at some of the gifts the Bible records:

■ Read Romans 12:6–8. List the spiritual gifts from this passage:

❑ 1)

❑ 2)

❑ 3)

❑ 4)

❑ 5)

❑ 6)

❑ 7)

■ Read I Corinthians 12:7–10. List the spiritual gifts from this passage:

❑ 1)

❑ 2)

❑ 3)

❑ 4)

❑ 5)

❑ 6)

❑ 7)

■ Read I Corinthians 12:28–30. List the spiritual gifts from this passage:

❑ 1)

❑ 2)

❑ 3)

❑ 4)

❑ 5)

❑ 6)

❑ 7)

❑ 8)

■ Read Ephesians 4:11–12. List the spiritual gifts from this passage:

❑ 1)

❑ 2)

❑ 3)

❑ 4)

❑ 5)

■ From the lists above, check the spiritual gift(s) you feel that the Holy Spirit may have given you.

day 19 > > >

Discovering Hidden Treasure

"There are different kinds of gifts, but the same Spirit. There are different kinds of service, but the same Lord. There are different kinds of working, but the same God works all of them in all men."

—1 Corinthians 12:4–6

Not only was William Randolph Hearst the rich and powerful owner of one of the world's most influential newspapers of his day, he was also an avid art collector. One day William found himself coveting two fabulous paintings he had spotted in an art book. He gave his staff the task of locating and purchasing the two works of art, regardless of the cost. After weeks of circling the globe in a no-holds-barred search, they were finally able to uncover the whereabouts of the two paintings. Amazingly, they were discovered to be in a warehouse located in the very city Hearst's newspaper called home.

Immediately upon receiving this information, William and his staff embarked on the final leg of their quest as they quickly drove to the address where they were told the paintings could be found. When they arrived, Hearst stared inquisitively at the building and said, "Wait a second, there must be some mistake. I own this warehouse and everything in it."

"There is no mistake," one of his staff members countered. "This is the correct address." Hearst sighed and remarked, "Then these paintings have been in my possession all along."

Just as those exquisite works of art were in Hearst's possession and at his disposal without his awareness of the fact, many Christians are unaware of the incredible assets that God has given them in the form of spiritual gifts. **So how do Christians go about *discovering* these Spiritual gifts God has bestowed upon us?**

1› You will be good in the areas of your giftedness.

Keep in mind, however, that you might not be proficient in using your gifts immediately because gifts can be developed. For instance, we had hands when we were infants, but those hands really weren't all that useful, were they? Every once in a while this appendage would come in and out of our vision, and we would lie there with this confused look on our faces and wonder, "What is that thing?"

After awhile, however, we would begin to grasp such things as dirt, bugs, and Sparky's dog biscuits to put them in our mouths. It was still awkward, but at least we were getting somewhere. As we matured, our dexterity and strength continued to upgrade, making our hands more and more useful to our body. Keep in mind that they have never changed from being hands. They have simply developed. That is why Paul admonishes Timothy to *"Fan into flame the gift God has given you..."* (2 Timothy 1:6).

2› You will love to serve in the areas of your giftedness.

Nobody has to psyche you up to serve in the areas of your gifts. That doesn't mean you'll be continuously excited. There isn't a teacher, regardless how gifted he or she may be, who wakes up every single day exclaiming, "Whoopee! I get to teach one more time!" Although I love preaching, there are days I probably would just as soon not. Moreover, there isn't a person who has served God in a ministry for any length of time who hasn't occasionally felt like giving up. But overall, there is a love and a hunger to serve in the areas of your giftedness.

3› Your gifts will be obvious to others.

Close friends who are spiritually mature can help point out your gifts. I don't have to ask my wife or dearest friends what their spiritual gifts are because I've seen them in action. I know their strengths and I know their passions. There are certain things I know that they love to do and live to do. Your friends will see your strengths and passions as well.

4> Take a spiritual gift inventory.

A spiritual gift inventory is a questionnaire in which you rate yourself on your various passions and abilities. Based on your responses, you can discover what spiritual gifts you may possess. Many good inventories are out there from which to choose. Fill out one or two and see how the results line up with these other ways to uncover your gifts.

5> Experiment.

Perhaps the greatest way to discover your giftedness is to try different ministries. When you do, you will discover that some areas of service definitely do *not* trip your trigger. For instance, I know one couple who, after their first week of volunteering in the church nursery, not only became blatantly aware they were not called to this kind of ministry, but they nearly took a vow of celibacy (and will never be able to use Dijon mustard on a hot dog again). On the other hand, there will be ministries that will touch your heart and soul to the point that you will want to yell, "That was sooo cool!" as you slap high-fives with complete strangers. We also know of people who have rocked a hundred bouncing babies, changed a mountain of dirty diapers, and sung one lullaby a thousand times in that very same nursery—and leave every week with a smile on their faces, warmth in their hearts, and a sense of deep fulfillment in their souls.

Once you begin to understand which spiritual gifts you've been given, you'll have a good indication of where God wants your service. Think about it: If you enter the military and your commanding officer hands you a submarine, chances are, the armed services intend for you to be in the Navy. If they hand you a fighter jet, that's a good indication that your C.O. desires for you to serve your country in the Air Force. If they sit you in a tank, one would suspect that the Army is your place. Likewise, if God has given you a particular spiritual gift, it is because He intends for you to be actively serving in those related areas of ministry. That is why Paul says:

"We have different gifts, according to the grace given us. If a man's gift is prophesying, let him use it in proportion to his faith. If it is serving, let him serve; if it is teaching, let him teach; if it is encouraging, let him encourage; if it is contributing to the needs of others, let him give generously; if it is leadership, let him govern diligently; if it is showing mercy, let him do it cheerfully" (Romans 12:6–8).

Knowing our gifts helps us answer several of life's most important questions, such as "What is God's plan for my life?," "What should my ministry be?," and "How should I spend my time and focus my life?" Every Christian is called to serve the cause of Christ, and our spiritual gifts indicate the particular ways are called to serve Him.

re**ACTION**

SPIRITUAL GIFTS TEST:

Imagine that you and a group of friends are in a dorm room preparing to devour a freshly delivered mushroom and opossum pizza (it's a Southern college). Suddenly, someone slaps the table hard in response to a hilarious NASCAR joke you just told, causing the pizza to fly into the air and land opossum-side down on the floor. Check the answer that best fits your response. You would say:

- ❏ "Sometimes our mistakes can be life-changing events..." (and twenty minutes later you end with a touching poem)—One of your gifts may be preaching/exhortation.
- ❏ "Let's order another one. I'm buying."—One of your gifts might be giving.
- ❏ "Don't kick yourself; it could've happened to anyone."—One of your gifts might be mercy.
- ❏ "Did you notice the aerodynamic principles displayed in the fall of that pizza?"—One of your gifts might be teaching.
- ❏ "Okay, let's get organized. Fred, start cleaning up the mess. Shelly, get another opossum. Bert, start growing mushrooms."—One of your gifts might be leadership.
- ❏ You didn't say anything, but started cleaning it up.—One of your gifts might be service.

■ List three ways you could use your spiritual gifts today.

1)

2)

3)

day 20 > > >

A Tale of Two Coins

"The world asks, 'What does a man own?'; Christ asks, 'How does he use it?'"
—Andrew Murray

"Now to each one the manifestation of the Spirit is given for the common good."
—I Corinthians 12:7

I have two 1973 quarters in my house. One is a beautiful "uncirculated" coin. The coin has no dings, no scratches, and no blemishes whatsoever because it has never been available for public use. It has also never done anything productive. The coin has never bought ice cream for a little boy or flowers for a young woman. It has never been used to procure tickets for a good movie or purchase medicine for an ill person. The coin has never brought one smile to one person's face or made a difference in anybody's life because it has never been used. On the other hand, my other quarter looks like it has been used as a chew toy for rabid gophers. While this coin may not be much to look at, I wish that baby could talk. It could tell us about all the ways it has been used to provide for people and to bless people's lives.

In the same way, you might be the most gifted person alive, but unless your gifts are "in circulation," the church and the world are no better off. That is why God tells us, *"Do not neglect your gift..."* (1 Timothy 4:14) and *"Each one should use whatever gift he has received to serve others, faithfully administering God's grace in its various forms"* (1 Peter 4:10).

The following are several other reasons why you and I should use our spiritual gifts:

1› Using my spiritual gifts reminds me that I was created for a purpose.

One of the biggest questions of life is, "Why am I here?" Is it simply to communicate, procreate, recreate, and then croak? Here is what your Designer and Creator says about why He made you: Ephesians 2:10 says *"For we are God's workmanship, created in Christ Jesus to do good works, which God prepared in advance for us to do."* In other words, not only were you created to know God and to love God, you were also created to serve God. And, the good news is, God not only called you to serve Him, He has also equipped you to serve Him by giving you spiritual gifts.

"The work of a Beethoven, and the work of a charwoman, become spiritual on precisely the same condition, that of being offered to God, of being done humbly 'as to the Lord.' This does not, of course, mean that it is for anyone a mere toss-up whether he should sweep rooms or compose symphonies. A mole must dig to the glory of God and a cock must crow."

—C.S. Lewis

2› Using my gifts reminds me that I am a vital part of a team.

In I Corinthians 12:12–27, Paul compares the church to a human body, and points out the significance of each part. Likewise, you are an important part of the Body of Christ. Imagine if your body had a role call:

"Lungs?"   *"Here."*
"Brain?"   *"Present!"*
"Spleen?"   *"Yo."*
"Bladder?"   *"I quit."*

Do you think such a decision for inactivity might have an adverse effect on the body? Of course it would. In the same way, the Body of Christ is affected by whether or not you are functioning in your gifts.

I have had many people express to me their feelings that because their gifts are more behind the scenes, they don't feel as though they are really making a contribution. But consider a football team for a moment. Although the quarterback and the running back might be the most visible members, that doesn't mean that the other teammates are any less vital.

If the center doesn't snap the ball to the quarterback, he's going to look pretty silly standing around in front of 50,000 people with his hands on some dude's rear. In addition, if the guard and tackle don't block for the running back, he is going to have a near-death experience when the middle linebacker cleans his clock. In other words, there is no such thing as an unimportant team member, and success is possible only when every member is using his or her gifts.

3› Using my gifts makes me a stronger Christian.

When I was eleven I broke my arm in a bizarre accident involving roller skates and square dancing. Quit laughing. I'm not making this up. I broke my left arm while attempting to square dance on skates. Two weeks after I got the cast off, I broke the same arm again in a not-so-bizarre bicycle accident. (There was absolutely no dancing involved in this accident. Okay, maybe a little "break dancing.")

By the time my second cast was removed, my arm had been immobile for several months. The difference between my right arm and my left was dramatic. My right arm was a huge, bulging, mountain of rippling muscle. My left arm, on the other hand, looked like a twig with skin. Okay, truthfully, the right arm looked skinny, but the left arm really did look like a twig with skin.

Similarly, just as we get stronger physically by exercising our muscles, we get stronger spiritually by exercising our gifts. Every time we step out in faith and use the gifts God has given us, we grow as a Christian.

4› Using my gifts is a vital part of me finding life fulfillment.

God gives us spiritual gifts primarily to bless and encourage others. However, because we each have an innate, insatiable need to be needed and to accomplish, investing these gifts also brings incredible satisfaction in our own lives as well. I don't think it is coincidental that the Greek root words for "gift" and "joy" are one in the same. Don't forget that "gift" and "joy" are linked. In other words, authentic joy doesn't come from making tons of money or from being popular. (If this were the case, Hollywood stars would be the happiest people on earth.) Instead, true joy and contentment are found in being used of God in the way we are gifted. I can testify that the most fulfilled and alive I have ever felt was when I was doing what I am created and gifted to do.

5> Using my gifts blesses lives and furthers God's kingdom.

God has bestowed spiritual gifts on us for a purpose: to bless, strengthen, and minister to His people and to His Church. This being the case, if we are actively using our gifts, we're helping the Body of Christ be all that it can be; thus, we are pushing the team forward, so to speak. If, on the other hand, we choose not to use our gifts, we are hindering the Body of Christ and holding back the team.

FUEL

"The man with the two talents also came. 'Master,' he said, 'you entrusted me with two talents; see, I have gained two more.' His master replied, 'Well done, good and faithful servant! You have been faithful with a few things; I will put you in charge of many things. Come and share your master's happiness!' Then the man who had received the one talent came. 'Master,' he said, 'I knew that you are a hard man, harvesting where you have not sown and gathering where you have not scattered seed. So I was afraid and went out and hid your talent in the ground. See, here is what belongs to you.' His master replied, 'You wicked, lazy servant!'"   —Matthew 25:22–26a

"Now it is required that those who have been given a trust must prove faithful."   —1 Corinthians 4:2–3

re**ACTION**

■ Which of your "talents" are you currently burying?

■ Which of your God-given "talents" are currently in circulation?

■ Fill in the blanks to this sentence:

During the next twenty-four hours, I can use my God-given talents and

gifts to _____

in order to be a blessing to _____.

day 21 > > >

McStewardship

> *"The professor of heaven and earth placed you here, not as a proprietor, but as a steward."*
>
> —John Wesley

> *"Realize that every material possession you have isn't owned, but loaned."*
>
> —Anonymous

I personally believe that one of the greatest gifts God has graciously bestowed upon humanity is piping hot McDonald's french fries. One memorable day, I drove my daughters to Mickey D's and purchased a large order of these golden brown potatoes for each of them. My mouth began to salivate as I watched them shamelessly snarfing down the hot fries without offering me so much as a sniff. Reaching a hand toward one of their deep-fried spuds, I asked if I could have a few.

I will always remember their answer. They said simultaneously, and I quote, "No."

"No? What do you mean no?" was my confused reply.

"No as in the opposite of yes" was their answer.

I quickly defended my intelligence. "I know what no means, I just can't believe you won't let me have any fries."

"But they're *our* fries," they retorted.

"What do you mean, your fries? I bought them for you. You wouldn't even have these fries if it weren't for me!" I stated passionately.

"We know, but they're still our fries," was their final defense.

Let me assure you that I did get some fries that day. I also received an important lesson on stewardship as well.

Sitting there in the McDonald's lobby, I began to understand how God must feel when we withhold from Him what He has graciously bestowed upon us. I began to consider that if I had chosen to, I could have taken away all of the french fries from all my daughters that day. Such an act was within my power.

On the other hand, I also could have bought fifty orders of fries and inundated the kids with greasy, yet tasty, potatoes. What my daughters didn't quite grasp that day was that every fry they consumed was a gift of their generous and strikingly handsome, yet amazingly humble dad. One of the greatest concepts we can grasp as believers is the fact that we don't own anything—we are simply the stewards or managers for the One who owns everything.

"God entrusts us with money as a test; for like a toy to the child, it is training for handling things of more value." —Fred Smith

Would it be hard for you to give $2,000 to a total stranger whom you just met and may never lay eyes on again? Before you respond, let me add one more ingredient into the equation that may totally alter your reply. What if you were the teller at a bank? Imagine this scenario:

Distinguished gentleman: "I'd like to withdraw $2,000 from my account, please."
Bank teller: "How about taking $400 instead?"
Distinguished gentleman: "I beg your pardon, I'd like $2,000 from my account."
Bank teller: "How about $450?"
Distinguished gentleman: "This is not an auction, my dear fellow. I want $2,000 from my account. I do have enough to cover that don't I?"
Bank teller: "Yes sir. In fact, according to our records, you own this bank and all of the money in this bank belongs to you."

Distinguished gentleman: "Then again—I would like to withdraw $2,000 from *my* account."

Bank teller: "I see your point. How about $475?"

Distinguished gentleman: "Which part of this don't you understand? This is *my* bank and *my* money and I would like part of it."

Bank teller: "But the money is in *my* vault."

Distinguished gentleman: "*Your* vault? Didn't you just say that this was *my* bank?"

Bank teller: "Yes sir."

Distinguished gentleman: "Well then, if this is my bank then doesn't it make sense that that is also my vault?"

Bank teller: "Well, I suppose, sir. But I'm standing in front of the vault. Shouldn't that count for something?"

Distinguished gentleman: "The only thing that you can count on is that you will be on the unemployment line if you don't give me my money!"

Bank teller: "I don't understand sir. Do you mean that even though I work at this bank and stand in front of this vault, that doesn't mean I control the money?"

Distinguished gentleman: (calming down) "That's exactly what I mean."

Bank teller: "I guess it's been in my hands for so long that I've started to think of it as my own."

Distinguished gentleman: "You *manage* the money. You don't own it or control it. You manage the money, but don't ever forget: *You manage the money for me.* It is my bank, my vault, and my money. Your job is to put my money where I tell you."

Bank teller: "Well, when you put it that way, that makes giving you the $2,000 easy, since it's your money anyway. Here it is, sir. Would you like any more? Can I be of any further service?"

Distinguished gentleman: "No, that should be sufficient for today."

Bank teller: "Thank you, sir, and have a good day. Say, would you like one of my calendars?" (gentleman looks back with raised eyebrows) "Excuse me, would you like one of *your* calendars?"

Distinguished gentleman: "Don't mind if I do. I think you're going to make out just fine."

Likewise, all of our treasures, our time, our talents, and even our next breath are on loan to us from God. Only after we have settled the ownership question are we truly free to live, to give, and to serve.

"Since we are only stewards of the possessions God has seen fit to give us, every decision we make relating to our possessions has a spiritual implication. I wonder sometimes what difference it would make in our spending if Jesus had to appear in bodily form to co-sign all our checks before they would be negotiable."   —Cordell Dick

FUEL

"Wealth and honor come from you."   —I Chronicles 29:12

"Everything comes from you, and we have given you only what comes from your hand."   —I Chronicles 29:14b

reACTION

"A tithe of everything...belongs to the LORD; it is holy to the LORD."   —Leviticus 27:30

"Will a man rob God? Yet you rob me. But you ask, 'How do we rob you?' In tithes and offerings. You are under a curse—the whole nation of you—because you are robbing me. Bring the whole tithe into the storehouse, that there may be food in my house. 'Test me in this,' says the LORD Almighty, 'and see if I will not throw open the floodgates of heaven and pour out so much blessing that you will not have room enough for it.'"   —Malachi 3:8–10

■ Do you tithe (give ten percent of your income/allowance to God)?

"The purpose of tithing is to teach you always to put God first in your life." —Deuteronomy 14:23 (*The Living Bible*)

■ If God truly owns everything (which He does), and if He has commanded us to tithe (which He has), what will your response be today in the area of tithing?

❑ "No, these french fries are mine. *Mine* I tell you!"

❑ "How about those Lakers?"

❑ "Lord, it's all your money in the bank, and all the fries come from You. I know that I am simply a steward of what You have entrusted to my care. So in obedience to You, the Owner, I gladly give You the tithe out of love, obedience, and a heart filled with gratitude."

How God Guides Us in Our Big Decisions and Daily Lives

day twenty-two >>> **listening to God's voice**
day twenty-three >>> **trusting God's guidance**
day twenty-four >>> **confronting life's distractions**

FUEL

section 7

day 22 > > >

Run Bobby, Stop!

"Men give advice; God gives guidance."
—Leonard Ravenhill

"Teach me your way, O LORD; lead me in a straight path."
—Psalm 27:11

Have you ever observed the amazing spectacle of sideline coaching at a Pee Wee football game? Due to some apparent wrinkle in the time-space continuum, poor little Bobby somehow actually manages to gain control of a kickoff. Instantaneously, he is bombarded with an overabundance of conflicting instructions:

Dad: "Cut left, Bobby!"
Grandpa: "Run right, Bobby!"
Grandma: "Sweetie, give those nasty Neander-thals the ball before you get hurt!"
Charles' Dad: "Pitch the ball to Charlie!"
Jimmy's Dad: "Hang on to the ball, Bobby!"
Mom: "Don't do drugs!"
Baby Sister: "They squibbed the kick and over ran their coverage! Sweep right, fake reverse to the other wingback, then juke 'em out of their athletic supporters!"
Older Brother: "You stink!"
Coach: "RUUUUUUUUNNNNNNNNNNNNNN...!"

So many choices, so many voices. What to choose, what to choose?

The chances are that many of you who are reading this book are facing some tough decisions. *Who should I date? Who should I marry? What college should I attend and what classes should I take? What career should I go into? Where should I live? Do I want fries with that? Should I change jobs? How many children should we have? Should I invest in money markets or mutual funds?* Not only do we face the grueling gauntlet of the deep decisions of life, we are also bombarded with a plentiful plethora of daily decisions. So many choices, so many voices. What to do, what to do?

The good news is that answers can be found. God greatly desires to guide us through both the common and the desperate decisions of life. **Here are some of the many ways in which God speaks to us:**

1› The Word of God.

This is perhaps the most assured way of discerning God's will for your life. Most of the guidance we will ever need has already been given to us in the Bible. If you want to build something, you go to the plans. If you want directions, you go to the map. God's Word is our blueprint as well as our atlas. The Bible is the ultimate advice column—not written by people who are as confused as we are, but by our God, who knows everything and whose advice is always perfect.

Some guidance found in the Word is crystal-clear and straightforward. For instance, you don't have to ask the questions, "Should I honor my parents?" "Should I 'five-finger-discount' the CD?" or "Should I lie to my boss?" because God has already given us His definitive thoughts and commands about such things. On the other hand, some of the answers we seek may not be laid out explicitly in God's Word, but the Bible can still help us discern what to do.

For instance, you probably aren't going to find a specific chapter and verse as to whether you are to marry Tom or Eduardo. (Personally, we'd go with Eduardo.) You will, however, find principles as to the type of person with whom God wants you to tie the knot.

"The Bible is God's chart for you to steer by, to keep you from the bottom of the sea, and to show you where the harbor is, and how to reach it without running on rocks or bars." —Henry Ward Beecher

2> Other people.

God often speaks to us through parents, pastors, teachers, guidance counselors, wise friends, and others. Although I have children of my own, when I have a big decision to make in my life I still call my dad as well as strong Christians. In fact, God says we are foolish if we don't heed the counsel of others. Proverbs 12:15 tells us that *"The way of a fool seems right to him, but a wise man listens to advice."*

Jethro gave Moses wise counsel, which made him much more effective as a leader. Esther listened to Mordecai's advice and the Jewish people were saved as a result. In contrast, Rehoboam listened to the abysmal opinions of his young, inexperienced friends rather than the astute direction of the elders and ended up dividing the kingdom. So be careful whom you choose as counselors. Furthermore, if the counsel you receive ever conflicts with Bible, reject the counsel and trust the scriptures.

"If you cannot listen to your brother, you cannot listen to the Holy Spirit."

—Virgil Vogt

3> God's still, small voice.

Sometimes we expect God to write a message to us in the skies and we miss His gentle whispers and internal nudges. Perhaps you see somebody sitting alone at school and something within you whispers "befriend that person," or maybe after you've just had an argument with your spouse you feel the tug to apologize. It just might be that the stirring you are feeling has nothing to do with the anchovy and artichoke pizza you had for breakfast and everything to do with the leading of God's Holy Spirit. But once again, make sure that those inner promptings never conflict with the Word of God.

4> Peace.

Colossians 3:15 tells us to *"Let the peace of Christ rule in your hearts."* I am told that the more literal translation of this passage would be "Let the peace of God act as an umpire to arbitrate and decide what you should do." In other words, if you have two equally good decisions, ask, "Which one do I have the most peace about?"

"God wants to bring us beyond the point where we need signs to discern his guiding hand. Satan cannot counterfeit the peace of God or the love of God dwelling in us. When Christ's abiding presence becomes our guide, then guidance becomes an almost unconscious response to the gentle moving of his Holy Spirit within us." —Bob Mumford

5 › W.W.J.D.

This is more than just a catchy phrase on a Christian's bracelet. Asking, "What would Jesus do?" is an awesome way to make both everyday and life-changing decisions. And by the way, the best way to know what Jesus would do is to study the scriptures in order to find out what Jesus did do.

"It is better to ask the way ten times than to take the wrong road once." —Jewish Proverb

"A wise man will hear and increase learning, and a man of understanding will attain wise counsel...." —Proverbs 1:5 (*New King James Version*)

"But when He, the Spirit of truth comes, he will guide you into all truth." —John 16:13

reACTION

■ In what areas of your life do you most need God's guidance right now?

■ Find a topical Bible or concordance. To which scriptures does it point you concerning the areas in which you need direction? What commandments or biblical principles speak to your issues?

■ Which Christian brother or sister could offer you wise, godly counsel regarding your struggles? Talk to that person today.

■ What would Jesus do if He were in your shoes and in your situation?

PRAYER starter

"Holy Spirit, guide my decisions. Confirm it in your Word and direct me to wise counsel."

day 23 › › ›

Eye in the Sky

"I am satisfied that when the Almighty wants me to do or not to do any particular thing, he finds a way of letting me know it."

—Abraham Lincoln

"This is what the LORD says—your Redeemer, the Holy One of Israel: 'I am the LORD your God, who teaches you what is best for you, who directs you in the way you should go.'" —Isaiah 48:17

Picture yourself lounging behind the wheel of that red convertible you've always dreamed of owning. The wind is whistling through your hair, and the stereo is thumping out the rhythms of your favorite polka. Adrenaline is fuel-injected into your veins and then...you decide to pull out of your driveway. You find yourself cruising down a country road. Your tires are squealing like pigs in a tornado as you deftly handle each turn. If you were any cooler, you could freeze water.

Suddenly, however, you find it necessary to slam on your breaks with the force of a Saturn V5 rocket as you encounter the mother of all eighteen-wheelers, plodding along at a sloth-like pace. Frustrated that your speed could no longer set off a decent motion detector, you look for a way to pass this behemoth. The problem is, you can't see around the truck. Every time you ease over to see if you can pass, you barely get back over in time to avoid a head-on collision. Due to your limited vantage point, you simply cannot pass this giant snail on wheels.

Now imagine that your cell phone rings. On the other end is the familiar sound of a close friend whose voice is barely audible over the rhythmic *thumpa, thumpa, thumpa, thumpa* of a helicopter blade. He says:

"Hey, buddy, I'm flying overhead in my chopper and I noticed you were having some trouble passing that big rig. I think I can help you pass. In about half a mile, there will be a straightaway and it looks like no cars are coming in the opposite direction once you arrive there. You'll be able to pass him with ease."

Obviously, a friend in the sky changes everything. Because of his perspective, he is able to inform you as to exactly what's coming up on the road, and when it would be the safest time and place to pass. If necessary, he can even offer several suggestions of possible alternate routes.

Our life is similar to that ride in the convertible. Our perspective is limited. We want to make good and wise decisions, but we can't seem to see around the trucks. We dart in and out of traffic, unsure of which direction to go and what roads we should take. God, however, is like the friend in the chopper. He has a much better vantage point. He is omniscient. That means He knows everything. That means He is fully aware of all the best routes for us to take and the perfect time for us to take each turn. He sees every pothole, every road construction, every dangerous curve, every detour, and every possible route that will come our way.

Not only does He know the course that would be best for us, He wants to reveal that path to us. He wants to guide us on this road called life. In Psalm 32:8 God says, *"I will instruct and teach you in the way you should go; I will counsel you and watch over you."* The fact is, God desires to guide us, but that doesn't mean we're listening. What, then, needs to happen for us to hear from the Lord so that He can "instruct and teach us in the way we should go"? Before we are able to receive His guidance, we must first recognize His voice. Imagine this scenario of a traveling businessman who receives a late night phone call in his room:

Phone: (Ring, ring).

Businessman's wife: "Hello, snookums. I miss my sweet woogums. How's my pooky wookie?"

Businessman: "Hey, who is this?"

Totally uncool. But don't worry, the chances of this happening are very unlikely. When your spouse or a close friend calls, you rarely have to ask who it is on the other end of the line, because you know that person's voice so intimately. How are you so familiar with your spouse or friend's voice? Did you read a book about it? Did you attend a seminar? No, you have spent so much time communicating with each other that you could distinguish their voice from a million others.

This is the goal: that we are so intimately acquainted with God's voice that we begin to distinguish His from the cacophony of other voices that vie for our attention and allegiance. It only stands to reason that those who converse regularly with Christ will have a distinct advantage in hearing from God over those who don't. Remember though, as with any relationship, this doesn't happen overnight. With time and communication, His voice will become as familiar as that of our closest friend.

"Deep in your heart it is not guidance that you want as much as a guide."
                                                                —John White

"The watchman opens the gate for him, and the sheep listen to his voice. He calls his own sheep by name and leads them out. When he has brought out all his own, he goes on ahead of them, and his sheep follow him because they know his voice. But they will never follow a stranger; in fact, they will run away from him because they do not recognize a stranger's voice."
                                                                —John 10:3–5

"[T]hose who are led by the Spirit of God are children of God."
                                                                —Romans 8:14

"Men and women, let me ask you, how long has it been since you've had an intimate conversation with Jesus Christ?" —Charles Spurgeon

re**ACTION**

■ Of the following, which best describes your relationship with God?

❏ "Hello, this is 911, do you have an emergency?"

❏ "Hello, this is Luigi's Pizza and Taxidermy. It's eleven on Sunday morning, this must be you, Fred."

❏ "No, you're definitely not bothering me. I know we just talked a few minutes ago, but I never tire of hearing your voice, my friend. Now what's on your mind?"

■ What is a problem that you don't know how to get around? Ask for God's help to direct you.

day 24 > > >

Let Me Put You on Hold

> "All heaven is waiting to help those who will discover the will of God and do it."
>
> —J. Robert Ashcroft

> "Since you are my rock and my fortress, for the sake of your name lead and guide me."
>
> —Psalm 31:3

Have you ever tried to talk on the phone and had either your children or siblings making enough noise they could be heard in distant galaxies? What's your response? Do you:

■ Superglue their verbal orifice so as to ensure they'll never make audible, or at least distinguishable, sounds again?

■ Calmly state, "Dearest relative of mine, would you be so kind as to refrain from articulating so boisterously?" or

■ Retort, "Would you please be quiet! I can't hear a word this person is saying."

Is the reason you're having so much difficulty hearing the person on the other line because he or she is not talking, is a poor communicator, or doesn't like you? Possibly. But a more likely reason is that our environment is dominating our ability to hear. Sometimes listening to God requires turning off everything else. We wonder why we aren't hearing from God, but let's be honest: Our lives are bombarded with so many voices that the only way God could speak to us is if He took out an ad on the TV, logged into a chat room, or sent us an e-mail.

C.S. Lewis wrote that, in our time, it's easy to avoid God. All you have to do is, "Avoid silence, avoid solitude, avoid any train of thought that leads off the beaten track. Concentrate on money, sex, status, health and (above all) your own grievances. Keep the radio on. Live in a crowd. Use plenty of sedation." **The first, crucial step necessary for hearing God's voice is spelled out for us in Psalm 46:10:**

1› "Be still, and know that I am God..."

Turn off the TV (yes, some televisions actually come with an "off" button), mute the stereo, shut down the computer, and let your answering machine get the phone. Find a quiet place, and still your heart and mind. You might be thinking, "I pray at meal times, while I'm on the way to work, when my team is losing, just before an exam, and right before I hit the hay. So why is it necessary for me to have a 'quiet time' with God?" While brief, on-the-fly prayers might be a wonderful indication that you are aware of God's presence and power in every moment of your life. Those "quickie" prayers cannot replace quality time spent alone with God.

Be prepared though. Don't expect that when you turn off the stereo, unplug the phone, and begin to pray that it will always put you in a state of peaceful bliss. When you're not used to getting quiet, often all the thoughts, worries, and problems that you've ignored or repressed come rushing out like kids off a school bus. Give it time. Ask Christ to hold every pressing thought and worry at bay so that you can converse with Him. Not only must we remove physical distraction, we need to deal with spiritual commotion as well.

"But when you pray, go into your room, close the door and pray to your Father...."   —Matthew 6:6

What other steps can we take to help enable us to hear from God?

2› Put your antenna up.

A low-tech friend of ours recently purchased a new digital phone. She complained that it wasn't working worth a flip, and informed everyone that she was going to return the obviously defective product. On a whim, someone asked her if she had the antenna up. She responded, "Antenna? What antenna?" Similarly, if you want God to lead you, you need to be intentionally attempting to hear from Him. Isn't this what Samuel was doing when he said, *"Speak Lord, I'm listening"* (I Samuel 3:10)?

3› Unfreeze the pipes.

David said, *"If I cherished sin in my heart, the Lord would not have listened"* (Psalm 66:18). I think that goes both ways. I believe that the pipeline of God's guidance can freeze over in a hurry through disobedience. Repentance is the fire that unfreezes the pipes and reopens the lines of communication.

4› Just do it.

God doesn't speak to us just to pass along information or because He likes to hear Himself talk. He speaks to us desiring an obedient response. Why would God reveal His will to us if He knew perfectly well that we would be unwilling to heed His direction? God doesn't enjoy wasting His breath any more than we do. God quit talking to Saul because Saul quit listening to God (I Samuel 28:15–16). Likewise, God will withhold information from us until He knows we are willing to do what He says. On the other hand, I believe the person most likely to hear from heaven is the one who comes to Him with this attitude:

- ■ "Lord, the answer is 'yes'—now what's the question?"
- ■ "Lord, the answer is 'yes'—now what do you want me to do?"
- ■ "Before you even speak, I want you to know the answer is 'yes.'"

"The Holy Spirit expects us to take seriously the answers he has already provided, the light he has already shed; and he does not expect us to plead for things that have already been denied."

—Paul E. Little

5> Don't have selective hearing.

We can't pick and choose between those things we want to obey and those things that really don't trip our trigger. Anyone with children knows that kids possess selective hearing. For instance, a parent could whisper the words "ice cream," "toy," or "Disney World" from a cave in Tibet and his or her child would miraculously materialize out of nowhere, fully attentive to each syllable uttered from Mom or Dad's lips. On the other hand, a parent can put a 50,000-watt speaker three inches from his or her child's ear and broadcast, "Clean your room now" and two minutes later the child will question, "Did you say something?" Likewise, if we are selective as to what we want to hear from God, then we are not really listening.

"Our feet need to be connected to our ears."   —Andy Lambert,
Ear and Feet Illustrated
(Pablo Picasso Edition)

"Now we know why Andy suffers from 'Athlete's Lobes.'"

—Lowell McNaney,
Strange Body Ailments Illustrated
(Norman Rockwell Edition)

Jesus may be asking Christians and seekers today the same questions that He asked the people in His day:

"Are you listening to this, really listening?" (Matthew 13:9, *The Message*)

Likewise, Jesus may be asking the church today the same question that He asked the churches in the book of Revelation:

"Are your ears awake?" (Revelation 3:22, *The Message*)

In fact, Jesus may be asking *you* that same question right now: "Are you listening, really listening?"

FUEL

"Why do you call me, 'Lord, Lord,' and do not do what I say? I will show you what he is like who comes to me and hears my words and puts them into practice. He is like a man building a house, who dug down deep and laid the foundation on rock. When a flood came, the torrent struck that house but could not shake it, because it was well built. But the one who hears my words and does not put them into practice is like a man who built a house on the ground without a foundation. The moment the torrent struck that house, it collapsed and its destruction was complete."
—Luke 6:46–49

"'Come with me by yourselves to a quiet place and get some rest.' So they went away by themselves in a boat to a solitary place."

—Mark 6:31b–32

reACTION

■ Rate yourself from one to ten (with ten being the highest):

_____ Do you really want to have God guide you, even if He tells you something you might not want to hear?

_____ Do you truly trust that God will lead you in what is best for you, even when what He says may not make sense to you?

_____ Are you really willing to be obedient to God, even if there is a cost or sacrifice involved?

_____ Are you intentionally listening to God by spending time in His Word and prayer?

■ What distractions in life keep you from hearing God's still small voice?

■ What are some known sins that may be clogging your pipes?

■ So, how did you do? What insights "struck" you? What actions do you need to take?

Victory Over Daily Struggles

section 8

day 25 › › ›

Yesterday's Lies

"Where you start out isn't nearly as important as where you end up."

—Joyce Meyers

A friend of mine graduated from college at the ripe old age of fifty-three. For the previous eight years he had been working toward his bachelor's degree while holding down a demanding full-time job, remaining active in church, and being devoted to his family. To show their pride and admiration, friends placed an ad in the local paper announcing his collegiate accomplishments. To do justice to such a tribute, the newspaper requested that his mother send them a picture of her newly graduated son. So she obliged and sent them a photograph from his high school yearbook. (That's right, a simultaneously hilarious and hideous thirty-five-year-old picture.) He had mutton-chop sideburns, a cheesy mustache, long greasy hair, a zit that could be seen from outer space, and a digestive-enzyme-green, polyester shirt. Only a handful of people even recognized him from this less-than-flattering photo.

Being a good chum, I naturally clipped out the picture to mock him mercilessly. (It's a male thing; ridicule is a true sign of deep friendship.) He didn't laugh. He didn't get it. My buddy insisted that he hadn't really changed all that much since those high school days. You see, his mother wasn't the only one who still had a thirty-five-year-old picture.

> *"Therefore, if anyone is in Christ, he is a new creation; the old has gone, the new has come."*
> —2 Corinthians 5:17

Many Christians may carry around new pictures of themselves in their wallets and purses, but they still carry around old pictures of themselves in their hearts. Although these dear saints have become new creations in Christ, old failures, previous disappointments, and past sins continue to haunt their present thoughts. Like yeast in bread, these tattered memories affect every area of their lives. These "photos" have robbed their joy, destroyed their dreams, and soured the sweetness of life. Like seeing Aunt Bertha in her two-piece leopard-skin bikini, the memories just won't go away. **So what do we do with these old "photos"?**

1> Let Jesus dispose of some photos in "File 13."

We all have some junk from our past that we need to allow Christ to crumple up, crush in the trash compactor, burn, and then throw away the ashes. The big question is how? How do we learn to see ourselves as who we are in Christ, not as who we were before Christ? How do we allow Christ to develop new pictures of ourselves and overcome our past?

To answer that question, let's talk about vacuums. Not the kind that removes Sparky's hair from the carpet, but the kind science professors talk about excitedly before bored college freshmen. One of the principle assumptions of physics is that "nature abhors a vacuum" (as do most men). Scientists know that in nature, when something is emptied of one thing, it will soon be filled with something else. Likewise, if our hearts are empty of the truth, the old lies come back to roost. If we don't regularly renew our minds with the truth of Christ, our minds become like an empty parking space at the mall the day after Thanksgiving—it won't stay empty long.

That is why Paul encouraged Christians to fill and renew their minds with truth: *"Whatever is true, whatever is noble, whatever is right, whatever is pure, whatever is lovely, whatever is admirable—if anything is excellent or praiseworthy —think about such things"* (Philippians 4:8). I thought in the past that Bible study and listening to preaching and teaching were the equivalent of homework for Christians. These were things I had to do because they were ultimately good for me—kind of like eating my vegetables or flossing. I have now come to see these spiritual disciplines as a big, lovable bouncer, able to kick out lingering lies that I simply didn't have the strength to get rid of myself. Perhaps our problem is that we have over-estimated our own will power and underestimated the power of the Gos-pel. Christ doesn't want to take us out of the world; He wants to take the world out of us.

"Let a man radically alter his thoughts, and he will be astonished at the rapid transformation it will effect in the material conditions of his life."
—Henry James

2› Let Jesus put a new face on some of our old photos.

Instead of chucking the whole photo album, realize that the Lord wants to redeem and transform some of those old snapshots. I know a lady who is a collaging fanatic. She takes aged photos, then cuts, pastes, and arran-ges them until the final product is a beautiful collage. In her skilled hands, old and sometimes even ugly photographs become lovely works of art.

What this woman does to photos with scissors and glue, Jesus does to broken hearts with the cross and His Spirit. He transforms painful pasts into miraculous ministries. He takes what the devil designed to destroy us and uses it for His glory and our good. I once heard a woman share a tes-timony about how she had survived a truly awful, abusive childhood. She was physically, sexually, and emotionally abused for many years. She shared that not only has our Savior healed her broken heart, He has also used her testimony to reach and minister to a great many women who have faced and are facing similar struggles.

We are left with a choice: either we cling to those embarrassing, pain-ful "photos" or we allow Jesus to deal with our negatives.

"As nothing is more easy than to think, so nothing is more difficult than to think well."
—Thomas Traherne

FUEL

"[O]ne thing I do: Forgetting what is behind and straining toward what is ahead, I press on toward the goal to win the prize for which God has called me heavenward in Christ Jesus."

—Philippians 3:13–14

re**ACTION**

■ Circle the biblical truth you now need to be the background music of your life.

"For all have sinned and fall short of the glory of God, and are justified freely by his grace through the redemption that came by Christ."

—Romans 3:23–24

"But God demonstrates his own love for us in this: While we were still sinners, Christ died for us."

—Romans 5:8

"In all these things we are more than conquerors through him who loved us."

—Romans 8:37

"Be joyful in hope, patient in affliction, faithful in prayer.

—Romans 12:12

"You were taught, with regard to your former way of life, to put off your old self, which is being corrupted by its deceitful desires; to be made new in the attitude of your minds; and to put on the new self...."

—Ephesians 4:22–24

■ Write the verse you chose on a slip of paper and strive to commit it to memory by the end of the day. Hey, this isn't homework. This is inviting a friend into your home.

PRAYER
starter

"Lord Jesus, thank You for giving me new life.
Help me when my old life tries to creep back. Fill
me with Your truth until the lies have no room..."

d a y 2 6 › › ›

Lies We Believe

> *"It is contrary to reason for a thirsty person to turn from a pure, sparkling mountain stream to quench his thirst at a stale, putrid cistern; yet that is what the human race does when it rejects God's truth and standards in favor of the devil's impure philosophies."*
>
> —Billy Graham

> *"There is no power on earth more formidable than the truth."*
>
> —Margaret Lee Runbeck

Imagine yourself as a sailor in the year 1491. You are about to embark on your very first voyage. You're sweating like a Sumo wrestler in a sauna and your knees are knocking together like... like... like two knees *really* knocking together. Adrenaline is coursing through your body. Why the terror? Because from the time you were able to crawl and spit up whatever babies ate in 1491, people have bombarded you with the lie that the world is flat. This lie has affected you in two powerful ways.

First, it has kept you in fearful bondage. You are plagued with the horror that if your boat were ever to venture too far off shore, you would go careening over the side of the earth and thus, not only be killed, but also miss all reruns of "The Beverly Hillbillies" for eternity. Secondly, this lie has kept you close to shore. This falsehood has compelled you to sail with the land always within your sight and has also prevented you from venturing out to explore new lands. In other words, by believing this falsehood, both your attitudes and actions are profoundly affected.

The vast majority of the world believed the world was flat. They didn't just think that the world was flat; they were utterly convinced that this was the case. It wasn't until Columbus dared to believe something different that you received another Monday off from work; moreover, the lies that held you at bay melted in the heat of the truth. Similarly, as long we hold incorrect beliefs about God, sex, money, relationships, marriage, and the like, we will be profoundly affected in our attitudes and behavior.

Here's the problem: When we received Christ, we were made new in our identity, but we hung on to the same corrupted, stinkin' thinkin,' lie-filled mind. Romans 12:2 tells us, *"Do not conform any longer to the pattern of this world, but be transformed by the renewing of your mind."* So how do we renew our minds? Do we just pray a prayer? Do we simply will to do better? No, we get rid of the old and put on the new.

Ladies, if you wanted to dazzle everyone with glamorous fingernails, what would you do? First, you'd get rid of the old polish by putting on that stuff that smells to high heaven and can easily burn a hole through pig iron. Then you would put on your snazzy new polish. Similarly, guys, if you were to give the old Yugo a new paint job, what would you do? First, you'd get your sister's fingernail polish remover and...no, wait. You'd take off the old paint, sand it down, and patch it up. Then and only then would you put on that new "Arrest Me" red finish. Likewise, we need to rid ourselves of the lies we have so gullibly accepted and fill our minds with the truth.

What are some of the lies we have believed? Try these on for size:

- "I can't change."
- "I must be beautiful to be lovable—and the world will dictate what is beautiful." (The big one society has dished out to females.)
- "Accomplishment equals fulfillment." (Society certainly convinces males of this one.)
- "It's my responsibility to change that person." (If you really want to make life miserable for you and for the one you love, this lie is just the ticket.)
- "Marriage is the solution to my problems." (Society's lie to singles.)
- "Divorce is the solution to my problems." (Society's lie to couples.)
- "As soon as I accomplish _____ or obtain _____ , then I'll be happy."
- "The most important thing is to be liked."
- "Nobody cares."

> *"Unused truth becomes as useless as an unused muscle."*
>
> —A.W. Tozer

We also excuse wrong behavior with lies. We know something is wrong, but we do it anyway because we rationalize the action with falsehood. For instance:

S I T U A T I O N : Your parents discovered that you drank at a party.
Excuse: "I wasn't the only one."
Lie behind the excuse: "God doesn't take sin seriously if a group does it."
Truth: Even when we sin along with everybody else, we are still personally accountable.

S I T U A T I O N : You tell a little white lie.
Excuse: "I don't see any harm in it."
Lie behind the excuse: "If I don't see anything wrong with it, then there isn't anything wrong with it."
Truth: Are you really setting yourself up as the ultimate authority for the entire universe? Aren't you the same person who had "Disco Forever" tattooed on his arm?

S I T U A T I O N : You're confronted with the opportunity to smoke pot.
Excuse: "I'll only do it this once."
Lie behind the excuse: "If I only do something once, there'll be no consequences."
Truth: Ask those with sexually transmitted diseases, pregnant teens, and, if you could, dead drug or alcohol abusers if there were consequences for first-time actions.

S I T U A T I O N : You view internet porn.
Excuse: "Who's going to know?"
Lie behind the excuse: "There must be a witness in order for an action to be deemed sin."
Truth: God sees. God knows.

S I T U A T I O N : You engage in premarital/extramarital sex.
Excuse: "But I love him/her."
Lie behind the excuse: "Emotions and hormones are more important than character and obedience."
Truth: Character and obedience are always more important than emotions and hormones.

The best defense against lies is the truth. We not only need to peel off the layer of lies with which Satan has twisted our thoughts and impacted our actions, we need to fill our mind with the truth of God's Word. Jesus said that when we are His disciples, then we shall know the truth and the truth shall set us free (John 8:31–32). When we get a check-up from the neck up, then we can transform our stinkin' thinkin' and the hardening of our attitudes. We will experience true freedom when we: (1) Stop believing the lies; (2) Start filling our minds with the truth; and (3) Begin acting on that truth.

"Christian thinking is a rare and difficult thing; so many seem unaware that the first great commandment according to our Lord is, 'Thou shalt love the Lord thy God...with all thy mind.'"

—Oswald Chambers

"Good thoughts bear good fruit, bad thoughts bear bad fruit—and man is his own gardener."

—James Allen

FUEL

"[Y]ou have taken off your old self with its practices and have put on the new self, which is being renewed in knowledge in the image of its Creator."

—Colossians 3:9–10

reACTION

■ Of the lies that were mentioned, which have kept you close to shore?

■ What's one of the biggest lies perpetuated by today's society?

■ How does that lie affect people's lives?

■ What are some other lies Satan has whispered in your ears that have influenced your attitudes and actions?

PRAYER starter

"Holy Spirit, let me hear Your undefeatable truth that exposes and defeats the lies of this world…"

day 27 > > >

Don't Let the Door Hit You on the Way Out

> "When we confess our sins, God casts them into the deepest ocean, gone forever. Then God places a sign out there that says, 'No Fishing Allowed!'"
> —Corrie ten Boom

He's still sitting on your couch. Okay, glued to the cushions is more like it. You've given all the non-verbal signals. You've yawned. You've put the kids in their pajamas and said, "You kids go to sleep. We'll be there in just a second." You've asked if he'd like a Coke for the road and mentioned the busy day you have tomorrow. Still, he continues to overstay his welcome. "Can I get your coat?" didn't work. You've brushed your teeth, flossed, and gargled in front of him, but there's no sign of him leaving. There he sits, snarfing down your last Twinkie while he drinks your milk straight from the carton. He came over for what you hoped was a quick visit, but now he won't go home. His name is Mr. Guilt and you can't seem to get his fat posterior region off your sofa.

Now, don't get me wrong. Mr. Gut Wrenching Guilt can be a useful visitor. He can function like the nerves in our fingertips that compel us to jerk back from a hot stove to avoid burning our hands. Similarly, Mr. Guilt

beckons us to jerk back from sin in order to avoid scorching our soul. Ol' Guilt has helped lead more individuals to Christ than Billy Graham. In fact, most of the truly horrible events in human history are because Guilt was *not* invited for a visit. We can attempt to whitewash our lies, disrespect our parents, and use our tongue as a Ginsu knife. We can choose not to reach out to the hungry, keep passing along gossip about our friend or co-worker, and view that internet site without remorse. We can do all these things as long as Mr. Guilt doesn't stop by, tug at our heart, and awaken the nerve endings of our soul.

You may not always like what Mr. Guilt has to say, but he performs a task that is vital to our spiritual health. The problem isn't that Mr. Guilt comes by for a visit; it's that he isn't supposed to be a permanent guest. Guilt has no other purpose than to turn us back to Christ. But after that, it's time for him to hit the road.

"The purpose of being guilty is to bring us to Jesus. Once we are there, then its purpose is finished. If we continue to make ourselves guilty—to blame ourselves—then that is sin in itself."

—Corrie ten Boom

Guilt can come to our hearts in two forms: conviction and condemnation. What is the difference between the two? Conviction is of God. It is His Spirit notifying our spirit that something is amiss. Conviction is a tool that God uses to keep us out of harm's way and to draw us back into His loving arms. Satan, on the other hand, brings condemnation in order to freeze-frame us in the past and keep us away from the arms of God.

Whenever you feel convicted, be thankful.

First: Be thankful that you serve a God who won't let you hurt yourself or others without sending you a wake-up call. Second: Be thankful that your spirit is sensitive enough to feel God's conviction. After all, there are some, the Bible informs us, whose *"consciences have been seared as with a hot iron"* (I Timothy 4:2). With a couple of shots of Novocain, a dentist can numb our gums and remove our bicuspid with a garden tiller without us so much as flinching. Likewise, the more we turn a deaf ear to the Spirit's promptings, the more anesthetized our hearts become.

For some, however, the opposite is true. Though they've responded to God's convicting tug, turned from their sins, and received Christ's forgiveness, they remain plagued by guilt and condemnation. They choose to stay in the prison of their guilt, shackled to the chains of their misdeeds, when all the while God has already pardoned and released them.

Do you still have that unwanted guest in your heart? Have you felt the pain of your sin, repented, and asked Christ into your life, but are still imprisoned by the guilt? Now is the time truly and completely to let guilt go.

"Psychiatrists require many sessions to relieve a patient of guilt feelings which have made him sick in body and mind; Jesus' power of spiritual and moral persuasion was so overwhelming that he could produce the same effect just by saying: 'Thy sins be forgiven thee.'"

—Malcolm Muggeridge

Write one of these verses on a piece of paper, stick it in your pocket, and commit it to memory.

"If we confess our sins, He is faithful and just to forgive our sins and cleanse us from all unrighteousness."   —I John 1:9

"Therefore, there is now no condemnation for those who are in Christ Jesus."   —Romans 8:1

re**ACTION**

■ Would you say you have a healthy conscience, an overactive conscience, or have some calluses developing?

■ What are the areas where you are feeling the tug of God's conviction?

■ Are there areas in which you have previously repented that still haunt and plague you?

■ Where and how would God tell you to "stop fishing"?

"You cannot live in His presence without repentance."

—Tommy Tenney

PRAYER starter

"Lord, I know You have forgiven me for
_____ , but I'm having trouble forgiving myself..."

d a y 2 8 > > >

Just a Spoonful of Trace Elements

We have all heard the horror stories concerning the miniscule amounts of confirmedly disgusting particles that our government allows to be found within the foods we consume. For obvious reasons, they never seem to include these additional "surprises" when they list the ingredients. Imagine groggily pouring yourself a heaping bowl of Captain Sucrose cereal and drowning it with the old two percent. Just as you begin to scoop in the first mouthful, however, you are instantaneously jolted out of your sleepy stupor by what you read on the side of the box:

Captain Sucrose INGREDIENTS:

Sugar: 88%
Corn syrup: 4%
Glucose: 2%
Partially hydrogenated dehydrated sucrose: 1%
Enriched Mononitrateriboflavinpixydustplutonium extract: 1%
Love Potion #9 (as a preservative): 1%
Natural and artificial flavoring (free-range tofu, partially defat-
    ted fatty tissue, lunar surface material, decaffeinated celery,
    low-fat lard, dirt): 1%
Artificial coloring (Preparation K, Kryptonite, "Just for Amphib-
    ians" hair gel): 1%
Rodent nasal hairs*
Fly larva*
Factory worker toenail*
Yetti scabs* (to prevent clotting)
Roach dandruff*
Non-classifiable insect pellets*

*Less than 1%

How comforted would you be by the fact that these surprise or "extra" ingredients compose *only* a minor part of your complete breakfast? It's similar to the story about the father who was concerned about some of the movies his son was watching. The dad expressed those feelings to the young man. The son responded with a nonchalant, "Oh, Dad, it's just a little bad." "I see," said the dad. "I'll tell you what—I'll go make some brownies for you, and we'll discuss the issue further." The son agreed, and the dad came back shortly with the piping hot treats. As the son reached for the tasty desert, his father said, "Son, I went out back and got some of Sparky's 'yard mines' and cooked them in the brownies. But don't let that bother you. I just put in a little."

Just as we wouldn't tolerate even a small amount of Sparky-enriched ingredients in our brownies, we shouldn't tolerate even a small amount of garbage in our hearts, minds, and actions. In other words, any impurity we allow into our lives affects every area of our lives. Even a little sin hinders our relationship with God and others, saps our joy, grieves our heart, and weakens our witness.

"A holy life is not an ascetic, or gloomy, or solitary life, but a life regulated by divine truth and faithful in Christian duty. It is living above the world while we are still in it."
—Tryon Edwards

Let's look at this in another way. I've seen a river die. Before you send for the men in the white coats to take me away, let me explain. When I was a boy, there was a crystal clear river running through the mountains of Colorado. A river so pristine that it almost begged you to jump in and frolic in its gurgling purity. Several miles later, however, this same river was so awash with pollution that anyone who would be crazy enough to wade in its sludge might glow for weeks or grow additional toes. So what happened? How did the river die? A little oil spill here, a few beer cans there, a trace of phosphates here, a dash of sewage there, and before long the pure water had turned into putrid filth.

As you begin your new life with God, it's important to realize that one of Satan's biggest desires is to contaminate your life. That's why God says, *"Keep yourself pure"* (1 Timothy 5:22). Our loving Lord gives us this command, not because He doesn't want us to have fun, but because He knows that if we allow a little filth here and a little defilement there to infiltrate our lives, we will find our souls being polluted just like that river.

"Saying 'yes' to God means saying 'no' to things that offend his holiness."
—A. Morgan Derham

Does that mean God expects us to live perfect lives? While God desires that we strive for perfection, because of our humanness we aren't going to live perfect lives on this side of heaven. However, I do believe that God expects us, through the power of His Spirit, to "clean up the river." That's exactly what they did with the moving sludge in Colorado. Not only have I seen a river die, but I've seen one come back to life. People in Colorado cleaned up their act and the river, dealing with the junk that was already in the water and prohibiting further polluting. While the river still isn't perfect, the intentional effort to decontaminate the water has been wonderfully successful. Through God's power and our effort we can strive to keep our lives pure and holy as well.

"Our progress in holiness depends on God and ourselves—on God's grace and on our will to be holy."

—Mother Teresa

FUEL

"As obedient children, do not conform to the evil desires you had when you lived in ignorance. But just as he who called you is holy, so be holy in all you do; for it is written: 'Be holy, because I am holy.'"

—I Peter 1:14–16

reACTION

■ How might a trace of bitterness or a smidgen of lust affect your walk with God?

■ What are the three most obvious pieces of junk floating in your "river"?

■ What are three things you can start doing today to allow God to clean up your "river"?

day 29 › › ›

Dude, You're Gettin' a 'Tude

Here's a practical joke I played on my grandpa. Okay, it wasn't actually me who played the joke, and, if you want to get technical, my grandpa was not involved whatsoever with this prank. Other then those small details, this is a completely true story.

My sister and I (okay, to be precise, I don't have a sister either) had noticed that Gramps had conked out on the couch in a deep sleep, so we decided to have some fun. We smeared a little bit of Limburger cheese on Grandpa's mustache and awaited his return from Slumberland.

Sure enough, as soon as he awoke, Gramps began to sniff the air with a pained look on his face. "This room stinks," he declared as he moseyed into the kitchen. Grandpa Fred (not his real name) pointed his snout (not his real nose), took another whiff when he arrived in the room, and exclaimed that the kitchen smelled as well. Finally, Grandpa went outside to get some fresh air, inhaled deeply, and once again getting a snoot full of Limburger fumes, shouted, "The whole world stinks!"

Many real people, like my fictitious grandpa, have a Limburger attitude toward life. They could receive a dozen roses and notice only the thorns. A negative attitude pollutes and diminishes everything they experience.

On the other hand, other people possess incredibly positive attitudes even in the midst of the most difficult situations. With multiple daughters, I've changed my share of high-octane diapers in my life, if you get my drift. After a few years of experience, I discovered how to make it through these toxic ordeals.

I began by placing the changing pad and the child on the floor. I would then proceed to put one of those highly perfumed baby wipes on my knee and snort that glorious aroma continuously and as though my life depended on it. With a new outlook, I then got down to business. Likewise, some people have a lilac attitude toward life. They can be smack dab in the middle of Stinkville and still declare that life is good.

"The world is a looking-glass and gives back to every man the reflection of his own face. Frown at it, and it in turn will look sourly at you; laugh at it, and with it, and it is a jolly, kind companion."

—William Makepeace Thackeray

These are some vital insights concerning our attitudes:

1› Attitude determines our approach to life and our quality of life.

We can see by the Limburger and baby-wipe illustrations that our environment doesn't determine our attitude. Instead, it's attitude that has a major impact on whether life gets the best of us or we get the best of it.

2› Attitude is a choice.

We can't choose our name or on which side of the tracks we are born, but we can choose how we respond to life. Paul says in Philippians 2:5: *"Your attitude should be the same as that of Christ Jesus."* Paul wouldn't tell us to have Christ's attitude if we couldn't choose to do so.

"At any moment in life we have the option to choose an attitude of gratitude, a posture of grace, a commitment to joy." —Tim Hansel

3› Positive attitudes can be learned.

In Philippians 4:12–13, Paul professed the incredible claim that he had *"...learned the secret of being content in any and every situation, whether well fed or hungry, whether living in plenty or in want. I can do all things through Him who gives me strength."* Notice that Paul *learned* to have this attitude; it wasn't something he was born with. Also notice that it was Christ who gave him the ability to transform his stinkin' thinkin'.

4› Attitudes are contagious.

We have probably all experienced how either a positive or negative attitude can spread like a virus through an office, team, or family.

5› Attitudes affect how we view life and others.

It is a fact of life that we will see what we are looking for. Seasoned shoppers will see every "SALE" sign, because that is where their attention is focused. An eligible bachelor will spy every pretty lady, because that is where his antennae are directed. In the same way, if you're searching for the bad in people, your job, or your church, you'll find it. If, however, you are a miner for the good in people, your job or your church, that is what you will discover.

6› Attitudes help us to better handle life's failures.

It's like the little boy who proclaimed, "I am the greatest hitter in the world." He then proceeded to throw the ball in the air and miss on three mighty swings. Undaunted, the tyke declared, "What do you know, I'm the greatest pitcher in the world." There are going to be times we strike out in life. Keep swinging with a positive attitude and you'll hit some out of the park.

"The longer I live, the more I realize the impact of attitude on life. Attitude, to me, is more important than facts. It is more important than the past, than education, than money, than circumstances, than failures, than successes, than what other people think or say or do. It is more important than appearance, giftedness or skill. It will make or break a company, a church, or a home. The remarkable thing is that we have a choice every day regarding the attitude we will embrace for that day. We cannot change our past. Nor can we change the fact that people will act in a certain way. We cannot change the inevitable. The only thing that we can do is play on the one string we have, and that is our attitude. I am convinced that life is 10% what happens to me and 90% how I react to it. And so it is with you—we are in charge of our attitudes."

—Chuck Swindoll

"Moses heard the people of every family wailing, each at the entrance to his tent. The Lord became exceedingly angry, and Moses was troubled."

—Numbers 11:10

How did the Lord feel about the people's stinky attitude?

"But while the meat was still between their teeth and before it could be consumed, the anger of the Lord burned against the people, and he struck them with a severe plague."

—Numbers 11:33

How did the Lord respond to these whiners?

re**ACTION**

■ How would the following people describe your attitude?

❑ Peers: _____

❑ Family: _____

❑ Friends: _____

❑ Coworkers: _____

❑ People at church: _____

❑ Fictitious relatives?: _____

"Lord...he stinketh..."　　–John 11:39

■ What gets you in a "Limburger"/"everything stinks" attitude?

■ What is the toughest thing you might face this week? What are you dreading?

■ How could an attitude of completely trusting in Jesus affect the outcome? What is God trying to teach you?

■ What are three areas where your attitude needs adjusting?

1)

2)

3)

"Whines are the products of sour grapes."　　–Grape Poopon

day 30 > > >

Hook, Line, and Sink Her

"God never tempts any man. That is Satan's business."

—Billy Graham

"I'm not going to eat Mexican food again as long as I live," your friend declares passionately. "I mean it this time! Never again!" she repeats emphatically. No sooner have these words passed her lips when you hear the unmistakable zip of fishing line being cast from its reel. Mysteriously, a piping hot burrito hovers within inches of your friend's nose. Reflexively, she pounces on the soft tortilla like a lioness on an unsuspecting gnu. A thunderous chomping sound is followed immediately by a flurry of activity whereby your friend is translated from your sight in a blur as you stare wide-eyed toward the sky. A pair of high heels and the faint scent of jalapenos are all that remain.

"Poor girl, she never could withstand temptation," you say smugly as you turn to inform her next of kin. Suddenly, you hear the unmistakable zip of fishing line being cast from its reel as a lingerie catalog mysteriously dangles before your eyes.

Satan is a lot like a fisherman. We are the prey. Temptation is the bait.

Just as an expert angler takes the bait and carefully wraps it around the hook, being ever so vigilant to conceal its deadly point, Satan will lure us with all sorts of things that appear yummy to our fleshly appetites. But make no mistake, there's always a hook. He doesn't feed our flesh because he likes us, but because he knows that in order to hook us, he must first let us nibble on something that appeals to our earthly nature. Never forget that ultimately he only wants to kill, steal, and destroy (John 10:10). Old Slew Foot is extremely crafty. He knows when we are most vulnerable and which lures will work best on each of us. And we all know how good he is at peddling his wares and how lousy it feels to be one of his trophies.

Here are some things you need to know about temptation:

- **You *will* be tempted.** When the Apostle Paul addresses the subject, he says in I Corinthians 10:13, *"when you are tempted"* not *"if you are tempted."* As long as there is a devil, there will be temptation. It goes with the territory of living in a fallen world.
- **It is not a sin to be tempted.** Jesus was tempted, yet the Bible is clear that He never sinned (Hebrews 4:15). When then does temptation become sin? When we act on the temptation. A fish can't help it if a lure comes plopping into its pond. It can, however, help whether or not it takes a bite.

"Tis one thing to be tempted, another thing to fall."

—William Shakespeare

- **You do not have to fall for the temptation.** I Corinthians 10:13 declares:

  "No temptation has seized you except what is common to man. And God is faithful; He will not let you be tempted beyond what you can bear. But when you are tempted, He will also provide a way out so that you can stand up under it."

Isn't that great news? First, God promises that He will never allow Satan to tempt you more than you can handle. Second, He pledges always to provide a back door, an escape hatch, a way out so we don't have to succumb to the temptation.

Insights into Avoiding Temptation

1> Stay away from the pier.

Fish are more likely to encounter lures in some areas than in others. A fish that wants to stay alive would be well advised to avoid those high-risk areas. Likewise, some people and places contribute to our temptations. As a new believer, I discovered that when I started hanging around strong Christian friends, the amount of temptations and the intensity of those temptations decreased dramatically. Moreover, as I steered clear of some of those places I used to hang out and started frequenting other (better) environments, I discovered that I completely avoided many of those same temptations I used to face daily.

"If you keep hanging around the pool, sooner or later you're going to get wet."
—Andy and Lowell

"If you keep showing up at a bakery, it's only a matter of time until you buy a pie."
—Lowell and Andy

"If you keep walking in a cow pasture, it's only a matter of time until you step in a pie."
—Andy and Lowell

2> Don't nibble the bait.

If Mr. Fishy quickly swam to the other side of the pond and retreated when a lure plopped in the water, he would never be a filet that evening. Danger would be averted. It's when Billy Bass starts swimming around the bait that he begins to think, "I'm just gonna take one nibble." One nibble, however, progresses into one bite that eventually progresses to one fish stick. In the same way, if we immediately tell Satan to get lost when he dangles his goodies, the danger is quickly diffused. If, however, we begin to toy with the idea of acting on the temptation, we will eventually find ourselves "hooked."

"Better shun the bait than struggle in the snare." —John Dryden

3› Resist the fisherman.

James 4:7 instructs us to *"resist the devil and he will flee from you."* Jesus resisted Satan's onslaught of temptation by standing on the Word of God. That's why it is so critical to get God's Word within us so that when Satan comes with his lies and counterfeits, we can combat him with the truth. Remember, when you're filled with the filet mignon of God's truth, Satan's green bologna somehow loses its appeal.

"It is easier to stay out than to get out." —Mark Twain

4› Rely on God's power.

Let's face it, if we were to combat Satan's temptations in our strength alone, we'd be toast. The good news is that God's Holy Spirit empowers us to say "No!" to the devil and "Yes!" to God. Never forget that we have the power of God's Spirit and His promise that we can overcome any temptation. Freedom in Christ sure beats being Satan's catch of the day!

"However big the whale may be, the tiny harpoon can rob him of his life." —Malay Proverb

FUEL

"For the grace of God that brings salvation has appeared to all men. It teaches us to say 'No' to ungodliness and worldly passions, and to live self controlled, upright and godly lives in this present age, while we wait for the blessed hope—the glorious appearing of our great God and Savior, Jesus Christ...." —Titus 2:11–13

"For we do not have a high priest who is unable to sympathize with our weaknesses, but we have one who has been tempted in every way, just as we are—yet was without sin. Let us then approach the throne of grace with confidence, so that we may receive mercy and find grace to help us in our time of need."
—Hebrews 4:15–16

reACTION

■ What area of your life is causing you the most "pier" pressure?

❑ The "materialism" pier.
❑ The "power" pier.
❑ The "sex" pier.
❑ The "pleasure" pier.
❑ The "peer" pier.
❑ The "internet" pier.
❑ The "drug/alcohol" pier.

■ What are some practical steps you can take to steer clear of the pier?

■ List three "hooks" that might be hidden behind the bait that you find most tempting.

1)

2)

3)

"God delights in our temptations and yet hates them. He delights in them when they drive us to prayer; he hates them when they drive us to despair."
—Martin Luther

day 31 > > >

Your Cheatin' Heart

"Jesus replied: 'Love the Lord your God with all your heart and with all your soul and with all your mind.' This is the first and greatest commandment. And the second is like it: 'Love your neighbor as yourself.' All the Law and the Prophets hang on these two commandments."

—Matthew 22:37–40

"We are a product of the sum of our priorities." —Lowell and Andy

Announcer: "Welcome to 'Daytime Trash TV,' the show where you can air your family's insane, dirty laundry on national television for the entertainment of millions. We are still swamped with e-mails about yesterday's show, 'Cross-dressing Squirrels and the Nuts Who Love Them.' But that's nothing compared to today's show. Our conscience-numbing, soul-sucking topic today is, 'Wives Confronting Their Cheating Husbands.' Let's welcome our host, Slimy Weasel."

Crowd: "SLIMY! SLIMY! SLIMY!"

Slimy: "Hello! Let's get to it. Billy Bob, before we bring out your wife, Sally Bob, tell us your side of the story."

Billy Bob: "Me and Sally Bob been married for five years now and we got nine wonderful children: Football Bob, Hoops Bob, Baseball Bob, Synchronized Swimming Bob, Wrestlin' Bob, Nascar Bob, Bowling Bob, Billy Bob, Jr., and our newest baby girl, Bob Sled. She was named after my grandmama."

Slimy: "Billy Bob, from what you've just said, you appear to have a typical family. Why don't you go ahead and tell us your side of the story?"

Billy Bob: "I'm not a cheatin' husband. I don't care what she says; I ain't never cheated on her in my life."

Slimy: "Billy Bob, I'm in your corner. But just for kicks, let's hear your wife's side of the story. Sally Bob, come on out and confront this lousy, no good, cheatin' husband of yours."

Sally Bob: "Billy Bob, I ain't accusin' you of being with another woman. I'm saying you love that sports channel more than you love me."

Billy Bob: "There ain't nothing wrong with lovin' sports, Sally Bob."

Slimy: "Is it true, Billy Bob, that you haven't spoken to your wife in two years except to ask her where the remote control is?"

Billy Bob: "Yeah, but I ain't never cheated on my Sally Bob."

Announcer: "Tune in at this time next week for the special update broadcast of 'Aliens Captured My Dog Sparky and Now He Don't Look Like Elvis Anymore.'"

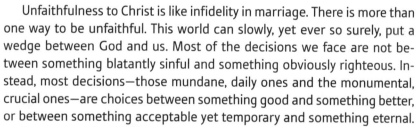

Unfaithfulness to Christ is like infidelity in marriage. There is more than one way to be unfaithful. This world can slowly, yet ever so surely, put a wedge between God and us. Most of the decisions we face are not between something blatantly sinful and something obviously righteous. Instead, most decisions—those mundane, daily ones and the monumental, crucial ones—are choices between something good and something better, or between something acceptable yet temporary and something eternal.

Remember the Old Testament account of the golden calf? Moses ascended Mount Sinai to receive the Ten Commandments and disappeared from his people's sight. The children of Israel, who were left waiting for Moses, grew restless and anxious, desiring to worship a god they could see and touch. In a great sin, Moses' brother Aaron helped the people build a false idol to worship. They melted down their gold jewelry to mold the calf, which they worshiped as a god. When Moses returned and confronted Aaron over this grave sin, here's the excuse Aaron came up with: *"I said to them, 'Let any who have gold take it off'; so they gave it me, and I threw it into the fire, and there came out this calf"* (Exodus 32:24).

What a brilliant line of defense: "I just threw in the earrings and out popped a false idol. It wasn't my fault, really." Although his excuse was pathetic, Aaron was right about one thing: Idols are created by surrendering one precious item at a time. Likewise, our idols are formed one decision at a time. If you took the things that are precious to you, the things you spend the most time and energy on each day, and set them in the fire of priorities, what kind of god would come out?

The Bible calls us to *"seek first the kingdom of God and His righteousness"* (Matthew 6:33). God doesn't say this because He's on a head trip, but because He wants to spare us heartache. False gods will always fail us. Therefore, if we put our focus, affections, or hopes on anything or anybody besides Almighty God, we will be doomed to disappointment. It is because He loves us that the Father calls us to put Him first. He is to be our first and greatest priority.

The question is this: What does it mean in your everyday life to make Christ your top priority? Today, the chances are you probably won't have to make a decision between bowing down to a golden calf and worshiping the one true God. You might, however, have to decide between going on a youth retreat and going to the Friday night football game. Tomorrow, you may decide between catching ten more minutes with the snooze button and investing ten minutes with your Heavenly Father. You'll soon have to make a decision between Bible study and reading the ingredients of the Captain Sucrose cereal box, again. Make no mistake—our everyday, priority-related decisions determine whether we will bow down to worthless idols or serve the Risen Lord.

"Feather by feather the goose is plucked."

—John Ray

"What is more, I consider everything a loss compared to the surpassing greatness of knowing Christ Jesus my Lord, for whose sake I have lost all things. I consider them rubbish, that I may gain Christ."

—Philippians 3:8

"But if serving the LORD seems undesirable to you, then choose for yourselves this day whom you will serve, whether the gods your forefathers served beyond the River, or the gods of the Amorites, in whose land you are living. But as for me and my household, we will serve the LORD."

—Joshua 24:15

re**ACTION**

Make two lists:

A) List the top five priorities of your life.

1)

2)

3)

4)

5)

B) In order of time spent, list yesterday's activities.

1)

2)

3)

4)

5)

The first list tells you what you want your priorities to be. The second list gives you a clue to what your priorities actually are. Pick one of the top priorities you listed above. How can you make that priority more of a priority?

day 32 > > >

Ask a Stupid Question...

"It need not discourage us if we are full of doubts. Healthy questions keep faith dynamic. Unless we start with doubts, we cannot have a deep-rooted faith. One who believes lightly and unthinkingly has not much of a belief. He who has a faith, which is not to be shaken, has won it through blood and tears and has worked his way from doubt to truth as one who reaches a clearing through a thicket of brambles and thorns."

—Helen Keller

"God has never turned away the questions of a sincere searcher."

—Max L. Lucado

"It is not as a child I believe and confess Jesus Christ. My hosanna is born of a furnace of doubt."

—Fyodor Dostoevski

Tommy raised his hand and began, "This might be a stupid question, but—" The teacher interrupted, "Remember class, don't be afraid to ask anything. There are no stupid questions."

Tommy, the teacher is wrong; there are plenty of stupid questions. Here are a few:

- If flies didn't have wings, what would they be called? Crawls?
- Why is abbreviation such a long word?
- If our knees bent the other way, what would chairs look like?
- Why do we park our cars on a driveway and drive our cars on a parkway?
- If you microwave instant coffee, would you go back in time?
- What's another word for "thesaurus"?
- What happens when you scare someone half to death twice?

See, there are stupid questions.

I met a young woman in college who loved to ask stupid questions. She would ask questions like:

- If God is good and all-powerful, why is there so much suffering?
- What about other religions?
- How can you say Christ is the only way?

Maybe I ought to re-phrase myself. Her questions weren't stupid. What was stupid was that she didn't really want answers. After talking with her several times, it was apparent that she was merely using her thought-provoking questions to justify her unwillingness to bow her knee to Christ.

Make no mistake: God is certainly big enough to handle our questions and doubts. I'll take someone struggling to know the truth over someone who just doesn't care any day. Devout Christians like Augustine and C.S. Lewis wrestled for years over the claims of Christ. So ask away. Seek the truth with everything that you have. The validity of Christ's message will stand up to every inquiry, but check your motives. Make sure that you are truly seeking answers and not just making excuses for disobedience.

"Doubt is not always a sign that a man is wrong; it may be a sign that he is thinking."

—Oswald Chambers

Do you remember the story of doubting Thomas? John 20:24–25 says, *"Now Thomas (called Didymus), one of the Twelve, was not with the disciples when Jesus came. So the other disciples told him, 'We have seen the Lord!' But he said to them, 'Unless I see the nail marks in his hands and put my finger where the nails were, and put my hand into his side, I will not believe it.'"*

We can overcome our doubts by doing what Thomas did. He brought his doubts to Jesus. In prayer, in Bible study, and in conversations with mature faithful Christians, we can bring our doubts to Christ. If your heart is unsure, the best plan of action is to strengthen your walk with Christ. Feed your faith and your doubts will starve. Remember, doubting Thomas became professing Thomas when Christ gave him enough evidence to unseat his uncertainties. He was able to declare emphatically, *"My Lord and my God!"* (John 20:28)

FUEL

"Now faith is being sure of what we hope for and certain of what we do not see."
—Hebrews 11:1

"And without faith it is impossible to please God, because anyone who comes to him must believe that he exists and that he rewards those who earnestly seek him."
—Hebrews 11:6

reACTION

■ What is the most pressing question that you would like answered? Ask a mature believer that question today.

■ What doubts or questions are you possibly using as an excuse or smoke-screen?

■ In what area of your faith might Christ say to you as He said to Thomas, *"Stop doubting and believe"* (John 20:27)?

"Christ never failed to distinguish between doubt and unbelief. Doubt is can't believe; unbelief is won't believe. Doubt is honesty; unbelief is obstinacy. Doubt is looking for light; unbelief is content with darkness."

—John Drummond

day 33 > > >

Super Christian

"In every Christian's heart there is a cross and a throne, and the Christian is on the throne till he puts himself on the cross; if he refuses the cross, he remains on the throne. Perhaps this is at the bottom of the backsliding and worldliness among gospel believers today."

—A.W. Tozer

"Peter asked, 'Lord, why can't I follow you now, I will lay down my life for you.' Then Jesus answered, 'Will you really lay down your life for me? I tell you the truth, before the rooster crows you will disown me three times!'"

—John 13:37–38

One week after Sam received Christ, the following comments were overheard: "Look, over there! It's a bird! It's a plane! It's Sam, the Super Christian! Able to leap tall sins with a single bound. With his X-ray discernment vision, he can see through the lies of this world. He can resist temptation without breaking a sweat. He can break a sweat without breaking a sweat. Able to witness passionately without fear or embarrassment. And he has a cape!"

Six months after Sam received Christ, the following comments were overheard: "Look, over there! It's a hummingbird! It's a kite! It's Sam, the mediocre Christian! Able to skip church in a single bound. With his normal vision, he's able to read the Bible, but amazingly he doesn't!"

One year after Sam received Christ, the following comments were overheard: "Look, over there. It's a dead bird! It's a plain, dead bird! It's Sam. Hey, why is Sam wearing a cape?"

Many Christians get discouraged when they discover that daily living can be the kryptonite for those who thought they were on the fast track to becoming "Super Christian." Not only can this discouragement throw us for a loop spiritually, it can even cause us to doubt whether anything authentic actually happened when we received Christ. Passion has been replaced by complacency and to our dismay we discover that, despite the fact we have accepted Christ, we far too often find ourselves behaving in very un-Christlike ways:

- The nagging habit that we thought had been evicted comes back for a weekend visit.
- We use our words to tear down rather than build up.
- Our prayer times become infrequent at best and non-existent at worst.
- We entertain thoughts that would better befit Charles Manson or Hugh Hefner than a child of God.

It doesn't take many stumbles to convince us that the big "S" on our chest stands for "Sinner" not "Super." As such, our state of mind could be summed up in three little words: "I give up."

Believe it or not, some of the giants of the faith have felt the same way. For instance, the Apostle Peter was, at times, a discouraged disciple. Here are the three little words Peter used to describe his discouragement: "I'm going fishing." After leaving his life as a fisherman, following Jesus for three years, seeing the crippled walk, the blind see, and the dead raised, being called "The Rock," drawing his sword to defend Jesus at His arrest, and after declaring emphatically, "I will never leave you," *Peter left Jesus*. To save his own skin, not just once but three times, Peter pretended not to know Jesus. Then he heard it: *Cock a doodle do!* A chill must have run up his spine.

A few days later, he abandoned Christ again with his words. This time, however, he didn't say, "I don't know him." He said, "I'm going fishing." With those three words he communicated the depth of his disappointment. "I'm going fishing," meant, "I quit. I'm not becoming the kind of follower I thought I would be. I keep messing up. I give up. I'm going back to my old life." His big boast had become a big bust. His faithfulness had flopped. His loyalty had lagged. His devotion had drifted. Okay, you get the point.

Peter wasn't the only disciple to flop. Judas blew it also. He traded his Savior for silver. Peter denied; Judas betrayed. Both men failed miserably.

The contrast between these two very human men was what happened after their failure. Although Peter must've thought he was off the team or at the very least condemned to the bench for life, he nevertheless chose to receive the forgiveness that Jesus offered. To his surprise, Jesus not only restored him to the team, but also put him on the first string. Peter went on to preach the Gospel, heal the sick, and author two books of the Bible. Peter, a forgiven sinner, also led thousands to a life-changing encounter with Christ by offering them the same forgiveness he himself had received.

Tragically, however, while this same grace was also available to Judas, he chose to wallow in his guilt rather than allow Christ to remove it. The Bible informs us that Judas "went to a tree and hung himself"—the ultimate "I give up."

Here's the bad news: We, like Peter and Judas, are going to blow it. In our own way we're going to betray and deny our Lord. Now mind you, we don't have to sin. God gave us His Holy Spirit to empower us to live godly lives. But the fact of the matter is that on this side of heaven, even the dearest of saints find themselves struggling with sin and even falling on their faces spiritually. (See Romans 7 for Paul's witness to this fact.)

So what's a sinner to do when he or she "hears the rooster crow" and is convicted of sin? Like our less-than-dynamic duo, we are faced with two options:

1) We can turn *away* from Christ and give up, or
2) We can turn *to* Christ, receive the forgiveness He offers, and get back in the game.

So what are you going to do when you hear the rooster crow?

"Success consists of getting up more times than you fall down."

—Oliver Goldsmith

"We must pay more careful attention, therefore, to what we have heard, so that we do not drift away."

—Hebrews 2:1

"My dear children, I write this to you so that you will not sin. But if anyone does sin, we have one who speaks to the Father in our defense—Jesus Christ the Righteous One. He is the atoning sacrifice for our sins, and not only for ours but also for the sins of the whole world."

—I John 2:1–2

re**ACTION**

■ Where is the rooster crowing in your life? (In what areas of your life do you feel God is giving you a wake-up call?)

■ In what ways have you "gone fishing"? (Is there an area of your walk with Christ where you feel like giving up or have already given up?)

"It's hard to slide on your back when you're resting on your knees."

—Lowell McNaney

"When you're resting on your knees, it's hard to slide on your back."

—Andy Lambert

"I just said that."

—Lowell McNaney

"You did not; you got the whole thing backward."

—Andy Lambert

"I didn't get it backward, you got it backward."

—Lowell McNaney

"I just said that.""

—Andy Lambert

"It's hard to slide on your back when you're resting on your knees, and when you're resting on your knees, it's hard to slide on your back."

—Lowell and Andy

PRAYER starter

"Jesus, although I realize I'm forgiven, I also realize that I still struggle with sin. Once again I turn to You..."

conclusion > > >

> *"The Christian walk is much like riding a bicycle. We are either moving forward or falling off."*
>
> —Bob Tuttle

The bottom line is:

The Christian life isn't easy, but it's worth it.
The Christian life is difficult, but God is faithful.

There will be times when...

- you'll face setbacks in your walk with God;
- you might not hear His voice or feel His presence, and you must trust in the faithfulness of His Word rather than the fickleness of your feelings;
- you'll be painfully aware that where God has called you to be, and where you find yourself to be, are miles apart;
- you'll find yourself taking three steps forward and two steps back, despite the best of intentions and effort;
- you'll wonder if you'll ever get it right or if you have what it takes to complete the journey.

You are not alone. Despite the fact that Paul was an Apostle, the Spirit-inspired author of most of the New Testament, a miracle worker, a world changer, and a hero of the faith, he nevertheless wrote:

> *"Not that I have already obtained all this, or have already been made perfect, but I press on to take hold of that for which Christ Jesus took hold of me. Brothers, I do not consider myself yet to have taken hold of it. But one thing I do: Forgetting what is behind and straining toward what is ahead, I press on toward the goal to win the prize for which God has called me heavenward in Christ Jesus"* (Philippians 3:12–14).

Notice these two things:

1) Paul confesses that he has not yet arrived nor does he have it all together.
2) His determination to strain ahead, press on, and, with God's help, never give up.

"We ain't what we want to be. We ain't what we gonna be. But, thank God, we ain't what we was." —Martin Luther King, Jr.

Take heart: God didn't create you to merely *start* the journey. He created you to *complete* the journey. God hasn't brought you this far in the journey in order to abandon you now. The same God who designed and destined you for a purpose, the same God who sought you before you knew Him, and the same God who saved you when you were helpless is the same God who will provide all the grace, power, resources, vision, courage, and all the hope you will ever need to complete the journey.

Never forget that you serve a

> sea-parting,
> > water-walking,
> > > sight-giving,
> > > > wall-crumbling,
> > > > > giant-slaying,
> > > > disease-healing,
> > > devil-delivering,
> > stone-rolling,
> death-defying Lord

who can handle any and every problem and situation and cannot and will not *ever* make a mistake or fail you. So

> rest in His arms,
> > sit at His feet,
> > > follow in His steps,
> > > > listen to His voice,
> > > seek His face,
> > know His heart, and
> receive from His gracious hand.

Jesus will provide all the fuel you will ever need for the journey, and He will be with you every step of the way. You never walk alone.

"Being confident of this, that he who began a good work in you will carrying it on to completion until the day of Christ Jesus."

—Philippians 1:1–6

If you have any questions or comments about this book, want to order additional copies, or want to find out about bulk order discounts, contact us directly by e-mail or in writing:

e-mail:
fuelforthejourney@hotmail.com

write:
Isaac Ministries, P.O. Box 275, Boonville, NC 27011

acknowledgments > > >

We thank You, gracious Lord, for the many people who made this book possible. We are especially grateful for our families, who allowed us to be away so often during the two years it took us to bring this baby to completion. We wish to thank and acknowledge the following individuals who were instrumental in bringing this book to print:

>>> *emotional support and unwavering patience:*
the unparalleled staff and congregation of Crossroads UMC, and the incredible supporters of Isaac Ministries.

>>> *housing:*
Dave and Karen Harper. Thanks so much for providing an inspiring refuge in which to write.

>>> *script editing:*
Serena Haneline
Rev. John Graham
Rev. Peter McGuire
Beth Gianopolis
Jana Alexander
Teresa Geiger
Rev. Jim Martin
Ken Kroemer
Nancy Friend
the late Sue Eble

>>> *hair and makeup:*
Martin "Chia" Luther

>>> *film editing:*
David Hockett

>>> *gaffer:*
Neill Shaw

>>> *wiring and electrical safety:*
Sparky

>>> *Sparky's trainers:*
Duke the Geniushound
Zoey the Wonderdog

>>> *photo retouching:*
Dan Hathaway

>>> *pyrotechnics:*
Paul Henke

>>> *liaison to the Swedish government:*
    Byran Shore
    Raymond Jones

>>> *key grips:*
    Rebecca, Cassie, and Aleia McNaney

>>> *boom operators:*
    Grace and Joy Lambert

>>> *security:*
    Brent Evans

>>> *ideas stolen from and duct cleaning:*
    Tim Martin

>>> *catering by:*
    Lois, Rita, Ray, and Peggy

>>> *musical accompaniment:*
    Tim, Susan, Meredith, and Kristen Lambert

>>> *best boy:*
    Dr. Todd Williams

>>> *accounting and taxidermy:*
    Scott "Carrot Boy" Worley

>>> *starring (in order of appearance):*

  >> *supermodels:*
      Jennifer McNaney
      Renee Lambert

  >> *Lenny from Enny:*
      Mark Carnes

  >> *Carlos the Monkey Boy:*
      Craig Luper

  >> *woman singing:*
      Angel Christ

  >> *boy eating hotdog:*
      Lee Ziglar

>>> *stunt doubles for Andy and Lowell:*
    Mel Gibson
    Barbara Walters

>>> *personal assistant to Andy and Lowell:*
    Milgar the Flatulent

>>> *thanks also to:*
    the governments of Ecuador and Sweden for the loan of a
    Global Positioning Satellite, the celery, and the prosthetic wart.

No venomous beagles were harmed in the making of this book.

about the authors > > >

ANDY LAMBERT is the founder of Isaac Ministries, an interdenominational ministry of evangelism and renewal. Through Isaac Ministries he serves as an appointed general evangelist for the Western North Carolina Conference of the United Methodist Church. Prior to his appointment, Andy was a pastor for ten years. He has had the awesome opportunity to proclaim the Good News of Jesus Christ in Mexico, England, Wales, Northern Ireland, and throughout the Southeastern United States. Andy is the author of *Man-Eatin' Mutant Monsters from Mars and Other Stories about Jesus.* He has taught "Fiction in the Christian Tradition" at Rockingham Community College and "Preaching to the Pierced Tongue" (a course on reaching youth for Christ) at Pfeiffer University. Reverend Lambert is renowned for his amazing nasal capacity and has the sense of humor of an extremely immature nine-year-old boy. He is married to Renee and they have two unbelievably wonderful daughters, Grace and Joy.

LOWELL MCNANEY is the founding pastor of Crossroads United Methodist Church in Concord, North Carolina. He has had the incredible privilege of proclaiming the Gospel of Jesus on five continents: in churches and cathedrals as well as in prisons, schools, and military institutions; in crusades numbering up to 150,000 people and in a shoe store with six dear saints; in the home of a Supreme Court Justice and under trees and huts in remote villages; before football teams and racing teams; in stadiums, on soccer fields and football fields, at youth gatherings and college campuses, and in hospitals, office complexes, modeling agencies, locker rooms, and on rooftops and dusty streets. Lowell is the recipient of the 1994 Harry Denman Evangelism Award. He loves sports, the outdoors, and people. Lowell considers himself the most blessed man alive as he is married to Jennifer and they have three unbelievably wonderful daughters, Rebekah, Cassie, and Aleia.

notes > > >

notes > > >

notes > > >

notes > > >

notes > > >

notes > > >

notes > > >

notes > > >

If you have any questions or comments about this book, want to order additional copies, or want to find out about bulk order discounts, contact us directly by e-mail or in writing:

e-mail:
fuelforthejourney@hotmail.com

write:
Isaac Ministries, P.O. Box 275, Boonville, NC 27011